The question posed by the person and w
I am?" continues to lie at the heart of C
collection, historical and contemporary
to revisit this enduring question and to ...
in a changing world.   ...p ... of Christ

Professor Elaine Graham FBA
Chair of Trustees, Modern Church

—

This is a vital and vibrant collection of essays for our time. For more than a century, progressive theology has been making substantial and valuable contributions to the field of Christology. Bold, engaging and intelligent, these new essays also provide us with fresh, new insights into the person and promise of Jesus, and his continued significance for the world today, and for all our futures.

Who is Jesus Christ for us today? These wise and perceptive essays offer excellent material for study groups, and for any individual wanting to engage with some of the major challenges we face in the twenty-first century.

Professor Martyn Percy
Harris Manchester College, Oxford

—

"Who do you say that I am?" The question Jesus put to his first disciples has to be faced by each successive generation. And it lies behind every page of this prophetic, passionate and sometimes provocative book. The wide range of responses it receives bears its own witness to the continuing global appeal of this first-century Galilean rabbi. Everyone with an interest in why Jesus matters in the violent, fearful, eco-conscious age we live in would richly benefit from reading it.

Bishop Gordon Mursell
former Dean of Birmingham Cathedral and former Bishop of Stafford

With attentiveness to historical and political as well as religious and interreligious considerations, *What Christ? Whose Christ?* gives expression to a polyphony of voices, bringing Christology into productive dialogue with feminist, liberation, Hindu, Buddhist, and other perspectives. The volume constitutes an important and provocative stimulation for further reflection on the significance of Jesus Christ in contemporary transnational and multicultural contexts.

Mikel Burley
Associate Professor of Religion and Philosophy, University of Leeds

What Christ?
Whose Christ?

New Options for Old Theories

— EDITED BY —

ALAN RACE

JONATHAN CLATWORTHY

Sacristy
Press

Sacristy Press
PO Box 612, Durham, DH1 9HT

www.sacristy.co.uk

First published in 2024 by Sacristy Press, Durham

Sacristy Limited, registered in England & Wales, number 7565667

British Library Cataloguing-in-Publication Data
A catalogue record for the book is available from the British Library

ISBN 978-1-78959-340-2

Contents

Foreword

"Who is this?" The question posed by those who witnessed Jesus stilling a storm on the Lake of Galilee has been constantly on the lips of successive generations. Those witnesses immediately answer their own question: "Even the wind and the waves obey him." Surely someone who could bend the elements to their will in such a way must be nothing short of divine.

"Is not this the carpenter's son?" This question asked by those who heard Jesus speak in his hometown of Nazareth entertains no such intimations of divinity. While they might wonder at how one of their own could speak and act in such a way, they were more inclined towards "local boy makes good" than, as a spoof sign on the entrance to Nazareth once put it, "local boy makes God"!

Such flippancy, of course, falls well short of the seriousness with which theologians have approached Christological questions, sometimes even violently. The American journalist, I. F. Stone, declared that "There's nothing more unholy in human history than a holy war—and no holy war has been more bewildering than that between the Arians and Athanasians in the fourth century." It was a battle fought over one Greek letter, the tiny *iota*, which could change *homoousion* (Jesus as identical in essence with God the Father) into *homoiousion* (Jesus as similar in essence with God the Father).

Identical or similar?—we've entered the world of classical Christology. And although the formula thrashed out at Chalcedon in 451 CE (stating that Jesus was both human and divine in one person) achieved a significant degree of consensus then, and for centuries thereafter, such questions never went away with a succession of "heresies" more or less successfully suppressed. Furthermore, today we have become more aware of the pivotal role that the politics of empire played in settling on the

Chalcedonian formula in the first place: no imperial power likes holy war spilling out on to the streets.

Stone went on to remind his readers that history lives on in the present, and although in relation to disputes about the person of Christ the debate today is conducted with rather more decorum, the issues at stake continue to divide Christendom. It simmers away and then occasionally comes to the boil. So it was that a conference was held in Girton College, Cambridge, in 1921 at which a distinguished roster of speakers aired what were adjudged by many to be dangerously radical views about who Jesus was in relation to God, and who Jesus is for Christians in the modern world.

Now, a century on from that controversial conference, Alan Race and Jonathan Clatworthy have edited a series of reflections, enabling voices to be heard which echo the Girton emphasis on the identity of Jesus in relation to centuries of cultural and historical change, but accepting that the impact of historical change and cultural awareness carry greater challenges to received tradition than was initially canvassed at the Girton gathering. Historical and contextual factors attend any doctrinal statements today, and here enhanced valorizing of rationality and experience in the modern world is promoted as key to the re-alignment of Christology if we are to ensure Jesus remains relevant and relatable. The Girton conference was organized by the Modern Churchmen's Union, as it was then called, and Mark Chapman's contribution in this book sets out the context of those times and its debates admirably. *What Christ? Whose Christ?* is sponsored by its successor, Modern Church, and the times could not be more different. Christological reflection can no longer be an isolated enquiry into the meaning of an ancient formula, but is learning to drink from the wells of historical consciousness, cultural criticism, feminist studies, and interfaith dialogue—perspectives all pursued in this book—if it is to make its mark.

This is not a straightforward endeavour. Should we interpret the figure of Jesus as either the best version of what it means to be truly human made in the image of God, or as a divine figure in-breaking time from the dimension of eternity? Is Christian belief in incarnation an invitation to imitate Jesus as a "parable of God's presence", and so indwell the world in godly ways? Or does Jesus represent a unique instantiation of God in time, inviting and inspiring our response in faith, and challenging us to entrust ourselves to the truth of "God in Man made Manifest", to cite words from Bishop Christopher Wordsworth's celebrated nineteenth-century hymn, "Songs of Thankfulness and Praise". By paying close attention to what can be gleaned from historical studies and believing that modern insistence on the full humanity of Jesus cannot be gainsaid, Alan Race's contribution leans inescapably towards the former assessment. Throughout the book we are invited to engage constructively with the decontamination of classical Christology in order to reclaim Christ for the modern church. The Enlightenment cannot be disinvented, and the melodies of critical studies cannot be drowned out by simply turning up the volume on old-time religion.

As the editors acknowledge, there is little focus in this book on solving the problem of how Jesus embodied two natures—one human and one divine—in a single person. This would be to contain the Christological task within limits too narrow to address contemporary contextualized concerns. So here we find at work the best instincts of theological liberalism: it entails a commitment to the creative re-presentation of Christian faith in forms and terms accessible and, therefore, available to modern culture.

One of the Christological issues raised under the influence of modernity, and faced head on here, is by Natalie K. Watson, whose feminist theology balks at the patriarchal language routinely deployed in Christian theology over the centuries and now no longer to be tolerated. Then in their contributions, Jonathan Clatworthy and Paul Hedges outline how such language is but one symptom of Christianity's historical recruitment by imperialist mindsets, when classical Christology effectively lost sight of the humanity of Jesus, notwithstanding its formal affirmation in the Chalcedonian definition. Consequently, dogma has all too often driven what men do to women, haves do to have-nots, Christians do to those of another faith or none, and those in power do to everyone else.

The Girton conference attracted a good deal of public attention at the time with its contributors routinely accused of hypocrisy, heresy and cruel assaults on the simple faith of the laity. The liberal tendency has never been other than subject to such criticisms but, as Clatworthy and Race point out, where its views have been contested they have almost invariably prevailed. Why? Because of three key characteristics: openness, honesty, and a mature relationship to the past. Openness is to truth, both in terms of where it might be found and where it might lead. It is not a prescription for indiscriminate allegiances or intellectual anarchy, and neither does it assume that liberal Christians engage with their faith without an accumulated store of knowledge and suppositional priorities—it's all very well having an open mind, but not at both ends! The openness we speak of is openness "to the possibility of a deeper Christian faith through modern understanding, in which the possibilities of faith are actually enriched through modern ways".[1]

Such a spirit demands total honesty. For example, the prescriptive claims that are often made for the sources of authority in the Christian religion, such as credal formulae, traditional practices, and foundational scriptures, are extraordinarily difficult to sustain in all honesty. There is now as great a need as there ever has been to be honest with one another when it comes to acknowledging the provisionality, or even fragility, of our credentials. Ecumenical and interfaith relationships can only bear fruit where this is the case, as the stimulating essays in this collection by Anantanand Rambachand and Mathias Schneider bear witness from Hindu and Buddhist perspectives respectively.

At the very least, we must be honest with ourselves as we seek to fathom the depths of meaning vouchsafed to us in the person, example, and teaching of Jesus. How often liberals have been so wary of overstating the transcendent otherness of Jesus that they have simply clothed him in their own humanity. The story is told of how one Oxford theology don asked a colleague if he had read the recent autobiography written by their head of department. "I didn't know he'd written one", came the reply. "Oh yes, he has. It's him to the life. Only for some reason he's called it *Jesus of Nazareth*." There is always the danger that what Christians have to say about Jesus tells us at least as much about them as him. These essays are impressive in their commitment to promoting Christological

---

[1]   Daniel W. Hardy, in Daniel W. Hardy and Peter H. Sedgwick (eds), *The Weight of Glory: A Vision and Practice for Christian Faith: the Future of Liberal Theology* (Edinburgh: T&T Clark, 1991), p. 300.

reflection which re-orientates the focus towards the humanity of Jesus without compromising that about his person and personality which has stimulated attributions of transcendence and the presence of the divine in and through him.

Finally, liberalism is strong on continuity with the past—in spite of efforts to malign it as otherwise—but it is a continuity that is more than mere reiteration. It is a continuity which ensures that the gospel is available to be heard in contemporary society. Those who went in quest of the historical Jesus did so out of the conviction that the Christian message could only be heard in the modern world insofar as it had been honestly subjected to the rigours of historical criticism. Claims to immunity from such critical analysis might secure for Christianity its own patch of high ground, but it would be high ground topped by an ivory tower delivering only megaphone messages to increasingly secular surroundings.

When the Christian message is made accessible to modern ears, with Christian ears open to the claims of critical thinking, then truth will have a chance to transcend the small-mindedness of religious triumphalism on the one hand, and rationalist exclusivism on the other. As this book demonstrates, when attuned to the tenor of a prevailing culture, Christians will find just how resourceful their faith can be in response, and it thus becomes possible, once again, for people to hear in their own tongue the good news of God in Christ liberated for a modern church in the modern world.

John Saxbee

Introduction

Alan Race and Jonathan Clatworthy

Jesus of Nazareth has always been a subject of controversy, both in his own lifetime and in his afterlife through history and culture. Aware that controversy is unavoidable, this book continues in the same vein, and in that anodyne sense is broadly traditional. But in many respects it is far from traditional.

The book falls within the area of Christian enquiry labelled Christology, that is, enquiry into the meaning of Jesus, his impact and identity. But immediately we should note that the very notion of Christology is less straightforward than we might wish for or has been assumed in the past. Interpreting Jesus as the Christ (in Hebrew, Messiah)—hence Christology—stretches from the narrow purpose of seeking to defend the two-nature doctrine that Jesus exhibited both human and divine natures in one person, finally agreed at Chalcedon in 451 CE,[1] to wide-eyed musing on the identity of the Jesus figure in relation to centuries of cultural and historical change. This book wholeheartedly embraces the latter perspective, believing that theological accountability is never static.

More immediately, the book has its origins in a set of lectures marking the centenary of the conference entitled "Christ and the Creeds", which was organized by the Churchmen's Union (now known as Modern Church) in 1921 at Girton College, Cambridge. The Union, as it was often called, began as a Church of England society "for the Advancement of Liberal Religious Thought", and for much of its history its name was The Modern Churchmen's Union (MCU). The word "Modern" was a gift from Pope Pius X, who in a 1907 encyclical had condemned

---

[1] See J. N. D. Kelly, *Early Christian Doctrines*, 5th edn (London: A&C Black, 1977; first pub. 1958), Chapter 12, here at pp. 338–43.

"Modernism" as "the synthesis of all heresies".[2] And for the MCU to call themselves "liberals" was a sign of resistance to both atheist and religious dogmatisms.

Intellectual developments from the nineteenth century, as they affect our theme, centred broadly speaking on two sets of ideas: first, on biological evolution in the wake of Charles Darwin's theory of natural selection;[3] and, second, on the deepening of the revolution in historical consciousness, with its ramifications for the historical study of the Bible. Both scientific evolution and historical consciousness were making their presence felt in theological and religious studies and affecting how we should be thinking about the doctrine of Christ and recitation of the Creeds. The Girton conference addressed these issues head-on. The conference caused a minor stir on the Anglican landscape and eventually led to the formation of the Church of England Doctrine Commission, which continues to this day. Many of its reports, however, have lacked the courage of critical enquiry which had surfaced at the Girton gathering.

At a deeper level, the conference witnessed a revival of the debate between "reason" and "revelation". For their first few centuries, Christian theologians openly debated their doctrines, and often with vehemence. Eventually what later became known as "Christian doctrine" took shape, with St Augustine (354–430) being the key synthesizing figure. The theologian Robert H. King summed up Augustine's role as follows: "More than any of his predecessors, [Augustine] succeeded in weaving together the various strands of Christian doctrine developed up to that point into a comprehensive and unified synthesis which could serve as the basis for future theological development."[4] Christian doctrine, which began as a lively developing product of the Christian imagination, after

---

2   Darrell Jodock (ed.), *Catholicism Contending with Modernity: Roman Catholic Modernism and Anti-Modernism in Historical Context* (Cambridge: Cambridge University Press, 2000), p. 1.

3   Charles Darwin, *On the Origin of Species by Means of Natural Selection* (London: John Murray, 1859).

4   Robert H. King, "The Task of Systematic Theology", in Peter Hodgson and Robert King (eds), *Christian Theology: An Introduction to Its Traditions and Tasks* (London: SPCK, 1983), p. 5.

four or five centuries became rather solidified once it assumed a shape as a "comprehensive and unified synthesis". King also called it a *paradigm* which would serve as the structure for most theological reflection in the West, at least until the Enlightenment".[5] By the end of the eleventh century, attempts were made to defend inherited doctrines rationally. The towering Western Latin figure, Anselm (1033/4–1109)—Archbishop of Canterbury (1093–1109)—for example, offered arguments that God existed, was a trinity, and was incarnated in a human. His arguments were widely challenged and by the time of the Reformation Protestants and Catholics alike were arguing that central Christian doctrines transcended human reason and had been revealed by God. Although there were exceptions, the dominant view was that the only things we can know about in matters of faith are what God had revealed—for Protestants, in the Bible alone, and for Catholics, in the Bible as interpreted by the Church.[6] Some, like Germany's Martin Luther (1483–1546), explained reason's limitations by appealing to the Fall of Adam and Eve in the Garden of Eden.[7] For Calvin (1509–64), nature still offered us some awareness of God, but humanity is so conditioned by sin that we could no longer read the book of nature rightly.[8]

By the early twentieth century, the divide between reason and revelation had been emphatically revived. Science claimed observation of phenomena and deductive reasoning as routes to knowledge and truth of the natural world, whereas theology appealed to scripture and revelation as routes to a different kind of knowledge and truth seen through the eyes of faith. The problem was, and remains, that knowledge and truth through faith seem less certain than the scientific outlook.

Refusing the "either-or" choice between new information and Christian tradition to date, the "liberals" and "modernists" argued that

---

[5]   Ibid.

[6]   The main exception was the Socinians, expelled from one country after another. See Bernard M. G. Reardon, *Religious Thought in the Reformation* (London: Longman, 1981), pp. 219–21.

[7]   J. C. F. Knaacke et al., *The Righteousness of God: Luther Studies*, 1883, 1.226, pp. 14ff. and 26ff.; Reardon, *Reformation*, pp. 80–1.

[8]   Calvin, *Institutes*, 1.6.2; Reardon, *Reformation*, pp. 183–6.

Christians had nothing to fear from modern knowledge. They believed that it was possible to defend religious belief rationally; that religious faith should be presented in ways compatible with modern science; that there was a proper role for evidence and personal experience in religious understanding; that non-Christian faiths had value as well as Christianity; and that central to Christianity was the human historical Jesus, not just the divine Christ of faith. Many now might wonder why there should have been a problem at all about these matters, but this reaction only indicates how much the modernist approach has succeeded in its determination not to descend into theological dogmatism or biblical literalism.

It is worth citing a parallel Catholic example manifest 20 years prior to the Churchmen's Union conference at Girton College. The French theologian, Alfred Loisy (1857–1940), wrote a line that has been cited many times since: "Jesus proclaimed the kingdom, and what came was the church."[9] That discrepancy between prediction and actuality was a dangerous one to make: it might undermine the credibility of Jesus as the saviour of the world. As a result, the Archbishop of Paris, Cardinal Richard, forbade Catholics to read the book. Loisy had pointed out a lacuna at the heart of Christian faith with its suggestion that Jesus predicted wrongly. However, more needed to be said. Loisy continued in the same passage: "a considerable change in the state of science (i.e. 'the general state of knowledge in the time and place where they were formed') can necessitate a new interpretation of ancient formulae which, conceived as they were in another intellectual atmosphere, can no longer say all that they need to, or do not say it as they should".[10] It was all too much for the leadership of the French Catholic Church and Loisy was condemned.

Loisy could easily have been a delegate at the Girton conference in 1921! What Loisy had alerted the Catholic Church to was being debated 20 years later by Anglican theologians. The present book continues this

---

[9]   Alfred Loisy, *The Gospel and the Christian Church*, tr. Christopher Home (London: Sir Isaac Pitman & Sons, 1904), p. 166.

[10]   Ibid.

spirit of critical enquiry first highlighted at the turn of the twentieth century and yet often still resisted at the turn of the twenty-first.

In the 1920s, among the doctrines that the Churchmen's Union debated, and largely doubted, were the physical resurrection of Jesus, the Virgin Birth, miracles and the realist and ransom doctrines of the Atonement. Their underlying principles can be summarized as follows:

- Christian beliefs change, and often need to in the light of new insights;
- new insights can be gained through research and from unexpected sources;
- the discovery process is open-ended and in principle democratic, rather than dependent on a pre-established authority structure;
- human rationality and creativity are not to be contrasted with divine revelation, but are valued as a means to receiving it.

The MC journal, in its early days, had two mottoes: one, attributed to Erasmus (c.1466–1536), was that "by identifying the new learning with heresy you make orthodoxy synonymous with ignorance"; and the other was from Edmund Burke (1729–97), who wrote that "a state without the means of some change is without the means of its conservation". This was the Modernist mood at the time of the 1921 conference on "Christ and the Creeds". Their opponents appealed to the teachings that the Church had inherited. As long as it was widely believed that human reasoning led to atheism, traditionalists felt the need for a divine revelation that gave answers transcending rational debate.

The conference provoked controversy as soon as it was announced. When Hensley Henson, then Bishop of Durham, heard of the plan to hold it, he wrote:

> I am persuaded that it will be grossly uncharitable and highly impolitic to thrust on the public notice exasperating and unproved theories about our Saviour, which cannot possibly be reconciled with the traditional belief of the Church, and which may be altogether incompatible with any living faith in Christ as

uniquely Son of God and Revealer of the Father. At this juncture a religious panic would be particularly unfortunate.[11]

Today it is difficult to imagine any religious conference attracting so much attention. The morning after the address by Hastings Rashdall, one of the conference speakers, *The Daily Telegraph* published a leader article saying:

> The Conference of "Modern Churchmen", now in session at Cambridge, is more interesting, and in reality more important, than a good many of the other conferences, whose "proceedings" congest the newspaper columns.[12]

However, as Alan Stephenson observed, "This sympathetic note was soon to be overshadowed by a great deal of abuse and criticism."[13] For example, the *Sunday Pictorial* on 21 August declared:

> There are some of us still left who believe in the divinity of Christ, and who totally fail to understand how men who believe the contrary can honestly occupy the pulpits of our State churches and take money for teaching people to deride the ancient faith.[14]

"Mordecai at the King's Gate", a correspondent to the *Western Morning News and Mercury*, declared:

> If it were possible for Arius, Pelagius, Socinus and Arminius to re-visit earth, these arch-heretics and anti-Christian preachers of erroneous and poisonous doctrines evidently would be welcomed by our learned theologians and spiritual guides.[15]

---

[11] Alan M. G. Stephenson, *The Rise and Decline of English Modernism: The Hulsean Lectures 1979–80* (London: SPCK, 1984), p. 112.

[12] Ibid.

[13] Stephenson, *The Rise and Decline*, p. 118.

[14] Ibid.

[15] Ibid.

In mid-September the conference papers were published. Opponents of the Churchmen's Union could then see that they were not at all as radical as many had claimed. (The same could have been said of Alfred Loisy.) But the controversy continued.

Henry Major, the central organizing force behind the Churchmen's Union, Editor of *The Modern Churchman*, and Principal of Ripon Hall Theological College, wrote in the October 1921 issue:

> A number of clergymen before they had read the conference papers wrote and spoke severely of their authors, and some, after they had read the conference papers, did credit to themselves and their order by publicly withdrawing their condemnations. The authors of the papers were described in Press and pulpit as "hierophants of heresy," "sceptics in the pulpit," "wreckers of the faith." Popular preachers regardless of the alarm they were creating, declared that the Christian faith had been shattered; others demanded that a definite repudiation of the conference utterances should be made by the Episcopal Bench and published in the secular Press; others urged that the National Assembly must lose no time in giving bishops power to deal with heterodox deans.[16]

Major was formally charged with heresy but the case against him failed. Nevertheless, Convocation, the governing body of the Church of England, heard complaints the following year. In response, a Doctrine Commission was established, but it did not publish its report until 17 years later—in 1938! The report generally exonerated the Modernists' position. However, by then nobody cared: Henry Major had ceded the limelight to Adolf Hitler.

Much has changed since 1921 of course. Both evolutionary science and historical studies have advanced and theological studies have had to adapt to new knowledge. What 1921 brought into the open was the legitimacy of critical approaches to received doctrines, and what was first greeted with alarm has slowly become absorbed within mainstream

---

16   *Modern Churchman* 11:7 (1922), p. 352.

theological studies. This was evident 38 years after that first Doctrine Commission report. In the Doctrine Commission Report of 1976 entitled *Christian Believing*, the then Regius Professor of Divinity in the University of Cambridge, the much-respected Geoffrey Lampe, wrote what for many has since become relatively uncontroversial:

> The breakdown of the concept of revealed theology has been caused largely by the application of the historical method to the study of doctrine and by the growth of the comparative study of religion. The great statements of orthodox belief formulated at Nicaea and Chalcedon are seen as products of their time, expressions of what Christians believed about the revelation of God in Jesus in terms of fourth and fifth-century philosophy. They are attempts, conditioned by the world of thought in which their authors lived, including its Greek theological presuppositions, to formulate insights derived from the Bible which had themselves been expressed in the forms of first-century Jewish and Hellenistic thought. They are not timeless expressions of truth communicated from heaven, but human attempts to analyse and describe inferences drawn from men's [*sic*] experience of encounter with God.[17]

We say "uncontroversial", but pockets of resistance were also present in that Doctrine Commission itself. Lampe's essay was not part of the main body of the Report and neither was the Report debated by the General Synod of the Church of England which had commissioned it, a sidelining move which itself revealed a high degree of anxiety at the level of ecclesiastical governance should critical approaches be allowed too much scope for making a difference to inherited doctrinal substance. If Lampe's view implied that received doctrines can no longer be taken

---

[17] G. W. H. Lampe, "Individual Essay 4", in A Report by the Doctrine Commission of the Church of England, *Christian Believing: The Nature of the Christian Faith and its Expression in Holy Scripture and Creeds* (London: SPCK, 1976), pp. 100–14, here at p. 103.

for granted, then what should Christians believe, including in the central area of Christology?

What Christ? Whose Christ? wholeheartedly agrees with Lampe's assessment of the impact of critical thinking on Christian belief, and in that sense fully recognizes historical and cultural contextual factors which attend any doctrinal statement today. His description of doctrines as "human attempts to analyse and describe inferences drawn from men's (*sic*) experience of encounter with God" could well have described the mood of the 1921 Girton conference on "Christ and the Creeds". Like Alfred Loisy, Lampe would have fitted in well as a conference speaker!

With pleasing serendipity, Lampe's citing of two crucial impacts from critical awareness—historical method and the comparative study of religion—concurs with the central intentions of this book. Let us now therefore turn to give a brief introduction to the essays themselves.

Although this book's chief aim is to explore Christological discussion as it is currently debated and accordingly to make its own contribution, the immediate groundwork for it was provided by the Modern Church's centenary marking of the 1921 Girton College conference "Christ and the Creeds". Therefore, it seems appropriate to grant the reader some insight into the historical circumstances of that conference, for as is often said in contemporary theological discourse "context is all". Mark Chapman fulfils this purpose admirably by placing Girton 1921 fully in the historical context of English Church life and ecclesiastical politicking, as well as developing trends and arguments in the theological thought of the period. Theological Modernism and Liberalism—and the two labels are indistinguishable at this period—had developed from the early years of the century with the aim of injecting critical responsiveness into theological developments and it functioned as a form of methodology in relation to those developments. But, says Mark, in marshalling some of those voices, the Girton gathering essentially succeeded in contributing to bringing about what amounted to an unplanned "third party" alongside dominant Anglo-Catholicism and rising Evangelicalism—in other words, a result more in line with ecclesiastical politics than with theological innovation.

This is not to say that there were no theological breakthroughs at all, but they were relatively muted in relation to what the conference seemed to promise. In general, believes Mark, "the speakers at Girton were seeking to restate the Christian faith in contemporary language rather than to question its eternal verities". Still, without doubting this overall assessment of the conference's intentions, a subtle philosophical issue remains: is it possible to forge contemporary language for even eternal verities without in some measure altering the meaning of those verities for their new context? If one surprise legacy from Girton 1921 was the identifying of a "third (ecclesiastical–theological) party", perhaps something similarly unforeseen had also been prized open—to borrow a well-known biblical allusion, does the new wine of critical faith properly also require the language of new wineskins? As a historian, Mark does not enter the philosophical dimensions of this discussion in relation to Girton, but further essays here do so in their different ways.

Jonathan Clatworthy presses the case that what he terms "imperialist theology" created a different wineskin with the adoption of Christian faith as the religion of the Roman Empire in the fourth century CE. As Jonathan puts it: "In a nutshell, when the Roman Empire became Christian, Christianity had to become imperial." And becoming imperial really did involve a subversive effect on Christianity's essential message. What began as a Jewish revolutionary religious vision and movement was reshaped into a pagan imperial faith that contradicted all that was central to Jesus's message of the Kingdom of God. Part and parcel of this reshaping was the development of what has been called High Christology, one of the essential issues at stake at the Girton conference.

Jonathan provides well-researched cultural and anthropological material as a form of cross-cultural evidence that the endorsement of imperial politics by religious metaphysics was a practice with deep historic roots and not confined to the ancient near east. Moreover, the development of High Christology was intrinsic to the subversion of early Christianity, which originally was based theologically and ethically within the Jewish egalitarian tradition of God's justice and the goodness of creation as in the first chapter of Genesis. One major effect of this whole developmental pattern was the essential loss, even eradication, of the humanity of Jesus himself, with the result that the main focus of Christian belonging turned "other-worldly", as witnessed in the Creeds. Again, as Jonathan puts it: "Christianity had to borrow the clothes of pagan philosophy which knew how to please emperors." The upshot at the Girton conference was that, perhaps even without realizing it, questioning imperial theology was not simply a philosophical matter but one that touched on the Christian soul itself if it was to reclaim a pre-imperialist faith.

If classical Christology effectively lost sight of the humanity of Jesus, in spite of its formal affirmation agreed at the Council of Chalcedon in 451 CE, Alan Race presupposes that the emergence of historical consciousness in the modern period places the human Jesus firmly at the forefront of any Christological enquiry for today. This is reflected in his deliberately provocatively chosen chapter title, "Does it matter if Jesus did not think of himself as divine?" Along with the majority of New Testament scholars it assumes that Jesus did not identify himself in that manner as such. But that has not prevented the tradition from depicting the human Jesus in countless divine terms through the centuries. However, the relativizing effects of the historical appreciation in so depicting Jesus in different forms can be amply illustrated through Christian art, as Alan demonstrates leaning on the work of Jaroslav Pelikan's celebrated achievement, *Jesus Through the Centuries: His Place in the History of Culture*.[18] However, countless depictions notwithstanding, this does not mean that an outline of what Jesus stood for, his parabolic teaching and practical impact, his religious purpose and effectiveness in the circumstances of his time, remains obscure. Once a historical outline is established, no matter how necessarily provisional, only then can we enquire into what this amounts to in terms of his "divinity" or what we might describe as the power and presence of God in and through him. Simply repeating past formulae, repeating even hallowed ascriptions such as "Messiah", "Son of God", even "Incarnation", does not take sufficient account of the interpretative element involved in any approach to the Christological task in a historically conscious age. Alan recommends making more use of the language of "parable" and "symbol" for interpreting Jesus in a culture that values "salvation" as the transformation of life itself, in both personal and structural senses. Furthermore, the possibilities for transformation will

[18] Jaroslav Pelikan, *Jesus Through the Centuries: His Place in the History of Culture* (New Haven, CT and London: Yale University Press, 1985).

also need to acknowledge awareness of movements such as feminism as well as the multicultural and multifaith identities that have shaped and continue to shape the world of the twenty-first century.

One discipline that has made a significant impact on Christological enquiry over the last 50 years has been feminist studies. Natalie K. Watson describes the changing perspectives of feminist theologians. Towards the end of the twentieth century, they discussed how the maleness of Jesus Christ affected Christian theology: how women were largely excluded from early Christological debate, and how Jesus's maleness had been used as a tool for oppressing women. Since then, feminist interest in Christology has somewhat declined, often because patriarchy has seemed unavoidable in Christology—or even in Christianity as a whole. For Daphne Hampson, if God is revealed as a male human, maleness has a status which no woman can attain.

In response, Natalie argues that being able to speak positively about Christ is too important, and has the liberating power that feminist theologians seek. Rather than rejecting Christology, feminists can respond by either reclaiming or reimagining the tradition. Reclaiming can take place through rereading early Christian literature to reveal a Jesus who "prefigures what redeemed humanity will be in an eschatological world of radical equality" or who perhaps was even a "proto-feminist". Or it can focus on Mary as a leader in a struggle for liberation, rather than the submissive woman preferred by patriarchal theology; or on the medieval women who have bequeathed to us their own experiences of intimacy with Christ; or on the recent art depicting Christ as a woman.

The task of reimagining Christology addresses the way symbolic language affects the lives of women. Toxic images of the masculine and feminine need to be deconstructed. Instead of asking what Christ did for us we should ask where Christ is with us.

The task of feminist theologians is to speak of God incarnate "in a way that enables women, and all of humanity, to flourish and to conceive of their own lives as being in the image of God".

Beginning in the nineteenth century, and intensifying through the twentieth, Western studies of the world's religions and interaction with leading voices have inevitably involved exchanges about the interpretation of Jesus in the light of new information and calls for more positive responses to global religious diversity. Two chapters in this book take up this challenge in relation to Hindu and Buddhist perspectives on Jesus. Both writers trace developments that generally chart a progression from suspicion, through a picture of mixed blessings, and towards a more positive dialogical relationship in the present, though the developments have been far from smooth.

First, in relation to Hindu traditions, the prominent scholar of Hinduism, Anantanand Rambachan, combines an early historic picture of Hindu–Christian relations, that were dominated by the context of European economic exploitation and political domination, with both an account from some of the major reformist Hindu voices in the early twentieth century (chief among them being that of the towering Swami Vivekananda, who mesmerized attendees at the 1893 World Parliament of Religions in Chicago with charm and erudition) and a personal narrative of the importance of Jesus for his own spirituality and understanding. On the one hand, Anantanand does not shy away from naming the negative side of Christian missionary activities, as when, for example, Christian voices either gave succour to colonial practices or announced the prejudicial superiority of Jesus and Christianity over Hinduism even prior to personal encounter with that tradition's significant voices. But, on the other hand, Hindu voices have mostly been welcoming of the Jesus story, especially when the focus of concentration was on the spiritual and ethical liberating effects of his gospel. There is much that can be shared and celebrated. The result of such positive rapprochement can be summed up in words from the revered Indian Christian theologian, M. M. Thomas: "If Christians can speak of an unknown Christ of Hinduism, Hindus can speak of an unknown Vedanta of Christianity."[19]

Anantanand shares the Hindu suspicion of Christian claims for Jesus as a unique mediator of divine truth. As he says: "My questioning in relation to Christian exclusive claims for Jesus must be seen in relation to the deeply rooted Hindu view that divine self-revelation is not limited even to the boundaries of Hinduism." This does not prevent him, however, from expressing deep appreciation for the God-intoxicated life

---

[19] M. M. Thomas, *The Acknowledged Christ of the Indian Renaissance* (Madras: Christian Literature Society, 1970), p. 150.

that Jesus exhibited and lived in compassionate concern for the poor and the neglected people of his time. In this sense, Jesus even challenges Hinduism if the latter's spiritual purpose remains fixed wholly on other-worldly transcendence. Still, Anantanand's overall verdict retains the difficulty: "Jesus's profound impact on me sits in unresolved tension with interpretations that appear all too often as arrogant and intolerant." But his moving personal account of what he terms "A Hindu *Darshan* of Jesus" (*Darshan* means seeing the sacred) overrides any negative judgements that Christian theology and ecclesiastical institutions may have made, and continue to make, on the worth of Hindu religious insight.

The book's second engagement with another religious tradition is with Buddhism. Although Anantanand did not canvas views of Jesus interpreted by some Indian dialogical scholars as an incarnated Hindu *avatar*, this is not the case with Mathias Schneider's essay, as can be glimpsed from the arresting title promising "a Buddha from Nazareth". As with Hindu responses, Mathias recalls the negative history of Buddhist responses to Jesus, mostly resulting, again, from the threatening impact of Western/Christian imperialism. But Christian engagement with Buddhism has been more fractious than with Hinduism, mainly because of the traditional Buddhist denial of a theistic God as the supreme reality. Mathias documents variable Buddhist responses to Jesus—as a "deluded deceiver", as a "Teacher of morality", and as a "Teacher of skilful means", that is, one who was capable of adapting profound truths to audiences shaped by cultural and religious forces of a lesser spiritual value. Beyond these historic interpreters, however, there are emerging others, mainly minority voices, who press the Buddhist case for more pluralist interpretations of religious life that create space for Jesus as *bodhisattva* (one on the threshold of nirvana but delaying entry for the sake of compassionate service of others), or even Buddha.

Mathias helps us to see how the scholarly Buddhist–Christian dialogue of recent decades has made numerous inroads towards establishing respect through open encounter, according the Other value in terms of spiritual insight and truth, and deepening the possibility of viewing Jesus as "a Buddha from Nazareth". This would not simply be a case of applying a Buddhist category to a spiritual teacher from a different cultural tradition, but of establishing convincing hermeneutics and philosophical epistemologies that open up the possibility of viewing Jesus and Buddha as two different manifestations of ultimate reality. Mathias then tests this potential breakthrough development against Christian beliefs in incarnation and crucifixion. In many respects one could say that the verdict remains open. For its acceptance, both Christianity and Buddhism will need to make considerable adjustments to their respective heritages, and Christology will remain a touchstone of credibility for either side. From the Christian side, Mathias questions if it is right that Christians insist "on a 'copyright' on Jesus".

What Christ? Whose Christ? is alert to the contextual realities of Christological explorations since the beginning of Christian faith, whether those contexts have been philosophical or socio-cultural. In contemporary theology, accounting for contextual factors has become a dominant concern. The chapter by Paul Hedges weaves a number of these factors, often tackled separately, together in a single cloth. The upshot is that contexts of antisemitism, anti-imperialism/colonialism, anti-racism, and liberation theology (tellingly from a Palestinian setting) converge to provide a devastating indictment against much that has passed for traditional Christology to date. It may be difficult to lay the blame for the ills of Christian praxis throughout the ages at the door of Nicaean and Chalcedonian interpretations of Christ, with the accusation that these interpretations *caused* so much suffering over time, but according to Hedges neither can they escape culpability. The effective eclipse of the human, material, and disturbing challenge of Jesus's message of the kingdom of God coupled with an overly concentrated orientation on his alleged "divinity" has rendered Christian faith powerless in the face of history's atrocities.

Paul's aim is to liberate Jesus "from the Latin, imperial, colonial, White, antisemitic, racist entrapment through which we so often receive him". He offers compelling reasons why this is necessary for Christological integrity, once we accept the cumulative critique arising from several contextual directions. In order to achieve this, Paul commends the view of the post-holocaust philosopher, Emmanuel Levinas, who believes that the Messiah does not come and that the messianic ideal passes to human beings as the agents to enact dignity, compassion, and justice for ourselves. Borrowing from and combining this with Palestinian theology,

Paul's Christological interpretation proposes that "the anti-racist Jesus of justice can reveal himself to us, but revealed in our own being and action". Whether or not this solution will be convincing for Christian faith in our time, it is certainly a view that deserves our serious attention, at the very least.

None of the chapters in this book have limited their sights to solving the problem of how Jesus of Nazareth embodied two natures—one human and one divine—in a single person. In fact, there are few Christian writers today who confine the Christological task within these narrow limits. A large part of the reason for this is that the impacts of historical and contextual studies have made their mark. As some of the writers here point out, even Nicaea's and Chalcedon's assessments were shaped heavily by political and philosophical factors that, in spite of their familiarity in theological education and liturgical recitation, are genuinely puzzling, even alien, when compared with twenty-first-century assumptions governing interpretations of reality. Thus even hallowed agreement from tradition cannot be free from criticism.

It has often been remarked that Chalcedon set the parameters for right belief in Christology, even though it failed to solve the difficulties that beset the debates of the early Christian centuries. But this approach, in the light of contextual studies, has now outlived its value as the single given focus for belief concerning the meaning and identity of the historical Jesus figure. The New Testament writer, Leslie Houlden, once noted that the long-held interpretation of Jesus as the incarnation of God is a likely victim too of the relativizing effects of historical interrogation: "[Strict incarnation] is a wonder, properly intelligible only within the patristic pattern where it found its articulation. Outside that pattern, if it is held, then it must be, I think, as a sheer wonder, a *magnum mysterium*, attracting faith and love, but defying reason . . . "[20]

But that is to jump the gun, ahead of wrestling with the issues raised by the individual perspectives of the writers in this book. Contextual Christology as it is practised today opens up numerous new horizons,

---

[20]   J. L. Houlden, "What to Believe About Jesus", in *Connections: The Integration of Theology and Faith* (London: SCM Press, 1986), pp. 123–38, here at pp. 137–8.

irrespective of one's view of incarnation, which anyway is capable of numerous adumbrations, ranging from the strict sense of the two natures doctrine to the general sense that Christian faith is an embodied faith concerned to maintain a unity between material living and spiritual vision. *What Christ? Whose Christ?* invites the reader into this exciting adventure in theological and Christological thinking. By recalling the Modern Churchmen's conference on "Christ and the Creeds" in 1921, it seeks to stimulate new investigations in the face of new challenges and different contexts more than one hundred years later.

1

The Girton Conference of 1921 and the Reshaping of Liberalism in the Church of England

Mark D. Chapman

This chapter discusses the Conference of the Churchmen's Union held at Girton College in 1921 which provoked a controversy in the wider Church of England on account of the Christological views of some speakers, particularly Hastings Rashdall and J. F. Bethune-Baker. It argues that although there was little that was particularly novel or unorthodox in the opinions expressed at the conference, it nonetheless provided the background for the setting up of the Archbishops' Doctrine Commission which reported in 1938. Against the background of a dominant Anglo-Catholicism and in dialogue with Stephen Sykes, I show how the Commission helped consolidate a theory of Anglican comprehensiveness which regarded liberalism as a party rather than a method. This served to limit its general appeal in the Church of England more broadly.

It is never straightforward to assess the importance of a historical event—any event will have not only a short-term effect but also a longer-term afterlife, which may be far less transparent and far less direct, and consequently less straightforward to describe and assess. This chapter seeks to discuss the longer-term impact of the controversies that flowed on from the Conference of the Churchmen's Union held from 8 to 15 August 1921 at Girton College, Cambridge. Its immediate effects have been relatively well documented: there have been several discussions of the debates over different topics in Christology that emerged from the

Conference. It is not my intention to enter these debates that worried some people—particularly some leading Anglo-Catholics—in the 1920s.[1] Instead I will look at the longer-term effects of the Conference on the broader development of the Church of England and its theology. What will become clear is that the Girton Conference occurred at a time when the partisan make-up of the Church was changing rapidly, and when increasing self-government following the Enabling Act of 1919 meant that parties were increasingly politicized as they were able to bargain for power within the new structures of authority, especially the Church Assembly, rather than simply as campaigning groups working from the outside. My contention is that the Girton Conference was particularly important in establishing the boundaries of a "third" party in the Church of England alongside Anglo-Catholics and Evangelicals.

The changed circumstances of the Church of England after the First World War meant that organized Church parties increasingly began to operate along the lines of political parties and could use the new representative institutions to bring about change even in such thorny issues as liturgical renewal or reservation of the Blessed Sacrament. The existing literature tends to treat the Girton Conference as a controversy about doctrine, especially over the nature of Christ, which was no doubt important, but it was also an aspect of the ways in which the different groupings within the Church of England sought to affirm their identities in the power brokering that inevitably emerged from the form of self-government that was adopted by the Church, which was modelled chiefly on the ultra-partisanship of the House of Commons. The changing dynamic of Church parties as they became more overtly political and depended on elections meant that the old squabbles which tended to take

---

[1]   See, for example, Alan M. G. Stephenson, *The Rise and Decline of English Modernism* (London: SPCK, 1984), pp. 99–150; Keith W. Clements, *Lovers of Discord: Twentieth Century Theological Controversies in England* (London: SPCK, 1988), pp. 85–106; A. Michael Ramsey, *From Gore to Temple: The Development of Anglican Theology between* Lux Mundi *and the Second World War* (London: Longmans, 1960), pp. 67–73; J. K. Mozley, *Some Tendencies in British Theology from the Publication of* Lux Mundi *to the Present Day* (London: SPCK, 1952), esp. pp. 84–6.

place through petitions to bishops as well as in courts and in campaigning meetings were increasingly replaced by a quasi-parliamentary form of institutionalized conflict that took place within the Church structures themselves. Although there had been many liberal-minded Anglicans over a very long period,[2] it is not clear that they had functioned as an organized Church party until this reorganization and reorientation of Church parties in the early twentieth century where they became a third force, usually referred to as Modernists or Liberals.[3] Through the decade they became increasingly consolidated as a rival to the historic parties that had emerged in the eighteenth and nineteenth centuries. The presence of this third party could in turn unsettle the uneasy balance of power that had emerged through the ritualist crises of the later part of the nineteenth century. The Girton Conference seems to have been crucial for the emergence of an organized third party in the 1920s alongside the increasingly self-confident Anglo-Catholics of the Anglo-Catholic Congress Movement[4] and the somewhat beleaguered Evangelicals who were prone to split over such issues as biblical inerrancy.[5]

---

[2]   See Mark D. Chapman, "Liberal Anglicanism in the Nineteenth Century", in Rowan Strong (ed.), *Oxford History of Anglicanism: Partisan Anglicanism and its Global Expansion 1829–c.1914* (Oxford: Oxford University Press, 2017), pp. 212–31.

[3]   The term "Modernist" was being used of those who associated with the journal *Modern Churchman*: see J. K. Mozley, *Some Tendencies in British Theology*, esp. pp. 48–9.

[4]   For more on this movement, see John Gunstone, *Lift High the Cross: Anglo-Catholics and the Congress Movement* (Norwich: Canterbury Press, 2010) and W. S. F. Pickering, *Anglo-Catholicism: A Study in Religious Ambiguity* (London: SPCK, 1991), pp. 41–64.

[5]   See David Bebbington, *Evangelicalism in Modern Britain* (London: Unwin Hyman, 1989), pp. 181–228.

The immediate impact of the conference

The immediate impact of the Girton Conference was perhaps somewhat unexpected. It was, after all, a small conference of a relatively new body held at the height of the summer. The Churchmen's Union under whose auspices the Conference took place had been established as a movement for the "Advancement of Liberal Religious Thought" in 1898.[6] It was a rather more establishment body than other liberal religious groupings such as those associated with the pan-denominational *Hibbert Journal* which was established in 1902 for scholarly interchange in "religion, theology and philosophy"[7] and *The Christian Commonwealth* which was first published in 1881 "to be liberal without being lawless: to be modern in our sympathies". It was later edited by the radical congregationalist R. J. Campbell, pioneer of the so-called "New Theology" which created something of a stir in the run up to the First World War.[8] Compared with those networks which had many Unitarian and other nonconformist devotees, the Churchmen's Union was both solidly Anglican and generally orthodox. In hindsight, the furore and uproar provoked by the Girton Conference which led to calls for heresy trials and recommitments to the Creeds by clergy were somewhat out of proportion to the content of the papers. In comparison with some earlier controversies, such as those provoked by the edited collections *Essays and Reviews* in 1860[9]

---

6   See Stephenson, *Rise and Decline*, pp. 52–77.

7   *The Hibbert Journal: A Quarterly Review of Religion, Theology and Philosophy* was published in London from 1902 to 1968.

8   On Campbell, see Peter Hinchliff, *God and History* (Oxford: Oxford University Press, 1992), pp. 198–222; Clements, *Lovers of Discord*, pp. 19–48; Brendan McNamara, "Eliding the Esoteric: R. J. Campbell and Early Twentieth Century Protestant Discourse in Britain", *Journal of Religious History* 43:4 (2019), pp. 511–30.

9   See Ieuan Ellis, *Seven Against Christ: A Study of* Essays and Reviews (Leiden: Brill, 1980) and Josef L. Altholz, *Anatomy of a Controversy: The Debate over* Essays and Reviews *1860–1864* (Aldershot: Scholar Press, 1994).

or *Foundations* in 1912,[10] it was rather less dramatic. This may in part be because, unlike with the earlier controversies, the leading personnel were hardly in their first flush of youth, and none could be described as an *enfant terrible*. The highest dignitaries that could be mustered were the aged canon of Ely and former headmaster of Clifton College, M. G. Glazebrook (1853–1926), the Dean of Carlisle, Hastings Rashdall (1858–1924), and the Cambridge Lady Margaret's Professor of Divinity, J. F. Bethune-Baker (1861–1951). The main controversy revolved around the contributions by the latter two. While both were undoubtedly eminent in their own fields, however, their notoriety hardly matched that of Hensley Henson following his appointment to the Diocese of Hereford in 1918.[11]

In many ways the Girton Conference was something of a repeat performance of the sorts of issues that had emerged over the doctrine of Christ in earlier controversies. It was much like the controversy provoked by the contributions to *Foundations* which had provoked some overblown reactions from the redoubtable Anglo-Catholic leader Charles Gore (1853–1932), Bishop of Oxford from 1911 to 1919, and Frank Weston (1871–1924), Bishop of Zanzibar from 1908 to 1924.[12] The debates over the person of Christ, sometimes concerning his resurrection, sometimes his virgin birth, and sometimes the very coherence of the incarnation itself, were matters about which many Church leaders grew anxious lest the Creeds should be watered down. The *Foundations* controversy was still raging at the outbreak of the First World War, and in many ways, it followed the pattern provided by the critics of the Broad Church tradition stemming from Benjamin Jowett and the writers of *Essays and Reviews* (1860), which functioned as a kind of manifesto for the Broad Churchmen. There had been a particularly vigorous outcry following its publication in 1860 which eventually ended up with the spectacle of a trial before the Privy Council. Ten years afterwards there had been attempts

---

[10] See Thomas Langford, *In Search of Foundations: English Theology 1900–1920* (Nashville, TN: Abingdon Press, 1969), esp. pp. 114–42; Clements, *Lovers of Discord*, pp. 49–74; Hinchliff, *God and History*, pp. 223–47.

[11] See Clements, *Lovers of Discord*, pp. 75–85.

[12] See Mark D. Chapman, *Bishops, Saints, and Politics* (London: T&T Clark, 2007), pp. 165–7, 211–15; Clements, *Lovers of Discord*, pp. 49–74.

to prevent the appointment of Frederick Temple, one of the contributors, as Bishop of Exeter. While the Broad Church movement had become an especially powerful intellectual force through the nineteenth century and into the twentieth century, it had never grown into a Church party, but influenced Church leaders across the parties, especially in powerful positions in the establishment (including Archbishop A. C. Tait and Frederick Temple).[13]

Sixty years or so later, the disputes over the Girton Conference were sometimes heated, even if the Church was left to deal with its own problems as the Privy Council had been relieved of authority in ecclesiastical causes. The pattern of complaint was relatively familiar: Church leaders of firm opinions grew anxious about theologians sliding away from doctrinal purity as they sought to make the Christian faith a bit more palatable to the "modern man". Especially prominent was the by now veteran Charles Gore, who had recently retired as Bishop of Oxford, along with a new breed of more extreme Anglo-Catholics including Charles Edward Douglas (1870–1955), co-founder with his brother John of the Society of the Faith and a strong supporter of the Eastern Churches. Any questioning of received doctrines they regarded as the thin end of the wedge which would mean the Church of England would lose its birthright of the inheritance of the faith of the apostles.[14] Once again, there were calls for clergymen to be made to declare their assent to the Creeds, with Douglas presenting a petition to Gore's successor at Oxford, the modern liberally-minded Hubert Burge (1862–1925), urging him to censure the speakers on the grounds of their questioning of the physical nature of the resurrection (which, after taking advice from the Oxford professors of theology, Burge refused to do). Similarly, there was a

---

[13]   See Mark D. Chapman, "Affirming Liberalism", *Modern Believing* 50:3 (2009), pp. 5–18, and more broadly, "Liberal Anglicanism in the Nineteenth Century", in Rowan Strong (ed.), *Oxford History of Anglicanism: Partisan Anglicanism and its Global Expansion, 1829–c.1914* (Oxford: Oxford University Press, 2017), 5 vols, pp. iii, 212–31.

[14]   On Douglas and the Girton Conference, see C. W. Emmet, "The Modernist Movement in the Church of England", *Journal of Religion* 2:6 (1922), pp. 561–76, here at p. 566.

presentation of a petition to the Bench of Bishops by the Anglo-Catholic English Church Union which called their attention to the "erroneous interpretations" about the Godhead of Christ and the doctrine of the Trinity exhibited at the Conference, which went on to ask the bishops "to declare that such opinions are contrary to the teaching of the Bible and the Church." As a result, the Convocation of Canterbury passed a resolution declaring its belief in the Nicene Creed in 1922.[15]

Despite these censures, however, it is fair to say that reading through the papers after a hundred years, it is hard to find much that would shake the foundations of the Creeds at least from a contemporary point of view: the controversy over the Girton Conference looks like a storm in a teacup, certainly in comparison with the lengthy legal trials following *Essays and Reviews*. Although there is a modicum of loose language here and there, in the lectures there is very little that would nowadays be regarded as heterodox, even by the most conservative scholars. In general, the speakers at Girton were seeking to restate the Christian faith in contemporary language rather than to question its eternal verities. As William Sanday (1843–1920), Lady Margaret Professor of Divinity at Oxford, who had adopted a more Modernist position from about 1912, had said in the fracas over *Foundations* shortly before the First World War: "I believe that the cultivated modern man may enter the Church of Christ with his head erect—with some change of language due to difference of times . . . without any real equivocation of his heart."[16] Such an approach well represents the Modern Churchmen of 1921 and is hardly cutting-edge radicalism.

Despite the often-heated debate, there were very few in the Churchmen's Union who sought a radical change of direction for the Church of England: such figures as R. J. Campbell with his New Theology were rare, at least in the mainline churches, and even he was eventually received into the Church of England during the First World War. Within the Church of England, the most controversial figure had been J. M.

---

15   C. W. Emmet, "The Modernist Movement", p. 567.

16   William Sanday, *Bishop Gore's Challenge to Criticism: A Reply to the Bishop of Oxford's Open Letter on the Basis of Anglican Fellowship* (London: Longmans, 1914), pp. 30–1.

Thompson (1878–1956), Dean of Divinity at Magdalen College, Oxford, who had published a book, *Miracles in the New Testament,* in 1911 which questioned the Virgin Birth and the physical resurrection, and which led to his licence being revoked by E. S. Talbot, Bishop of Winchester.[17] From today's perspective, the 1921 Girton Conference reads as a snapshot of theological debate and controversy which is shrouded in the presuppositions and language of the times. In many ways, the papers represent very little that was particularly novel. Apart from a modest recognition of the impact of an eschatological interpretation of Jesus's teaching on the Kingdom of God that had been espoused before the First World War by Johannes Weiss and Albert Schweitzer,[18] there was remarkably little that located the essays in the post-war context of reconstruction. Indeed, they are firmly located in the moderate liberal Protestantism of the pre-war world as well as the dominant idealist philosophy that continued to dominate Oxford and Cambridge. As I have already noted, the two papers that created the greatest stir were by Hastings Rashdall, in many ways the elder statesman of liberal theology, on "Christ as Logos and Son of God",[19] and J. F. Bethune-Baker on "Jesus as both Human and Divine".[20] Rashdall's paper developed a kind of late idealist degree Christology to try to translate the terms of traditional doctrine into (relatively) modern thought.[21] Similarly, Bethune-Baker's paper was far from radical even if his terminology was a little more likely to provoke: "I say my conception of God is formed by my conception

---

[17] Langford, *In Search of Foundations*, pp. 124–5. See also Daniel Inman, *The Making of Modern English Theology: God and the Academy at Oxford 1833–1945* (Minneapolis, MN: Fortress Press, 2014), esp. pp. 168–9.

[18] C. W. Emmet, "What do we know of Jesus?", *Modern Churchman* 11 (1921), pp. 213–28. See Mark D. Chapman, *The Coming Crisis: The Impact of Eschatology on Theology in Edwardian England* (Sheffield: Sheffield Academic Press, 2001).

[19] Hastings Rashdall, "Christ as Logos and Son of God", *Modern Churchman* 11 (1921), pp. 278–86.

[20] J. F. Bethune-Baker, "Jesus as both Human and Divine", *Modern Churchman* 11 (1921), pp. 287–301.

[21] Rashdall, "Christ as Logos and Son of God", p. 286.

of Jesus. The God I recognize is a supreme 'person' like Jesus in all that makes 'personality'. . . . So Jesus is the creator of my God."[22] Despite such occasional provocations, however, most of the speakers were far more concerned with defending a (liberally expressed) form of orthodoxy against the more extreme form that had been outlined by F. J. Foakes-Jackson and Kirrsopp Lake in their controversial book *The Beginnings of Christianity* published in 1920, which downplayed the novelty and the religious genius of Jesus Christ and was undoubtedly far more shocking to ordinary believers.[23]

The shared educational background of almost all of the speakers in the elite educational institutions of Victorian and Edwardian England and the underlying liberal imperialist ethos of progress and development are all pervasive through most of the papers:[24] the Platonist tradition of a ladder of perfection, for instance, shaped Rashdall's own approach to Christology and had implications for the way in which Christology related to Empire as nations themselves were sometimes ranked in relation to their degree of "maturity" in their capacity to grasp the divine.[25] In his introduction to the Girton Conference papers, for instance, Henry Major made this imperial connection clear. Major, who was the mastermind behind the Conference and the leading organizer of the Churchmen's Union, was also editor of their journal *Modern Churchman*. He served as principal of Ripon Hall, which had moved to Oxford after the First World War and had become a theological college designed to promote liberal theology to ordinands. He wrote that by discarding unnecessary doctrinal accretions there would be a new possibility for a truce between

---

[22]   Bethune-Baker, "Jesus as both Human and Divine", p. 301.

[23]   F. J. Foakes-Jackson and Kirrsopp Lake, *The Beginnings of Christianity* (London: Macmillan, 1920).

[24]   Rashdall had expressed some deeply racialist views. See Gary J. Dorrien, "Idealistic Ordering: Hastings Rashdall, Post-Kantian Idealism, and Anglican Liberal Theology", *Anglican and Episcopal History* 82:5 (2013), pp. 289–317, esp. p. 303.

[25]   See Mark D. Chapman, "Exporting Godliness: The Church, Education and 'Higher Civilization' in the British Empire from the late Nineteenth Century", *Studies in Church History* 55 (Churches and Education, 2019), pp. 381–409.

the denominations so that reunion could be achieved at home. This would mean that "Christian civilization" could be built up in India and the East, and the new generation of English men and women could be won. To do all this would require shedding something of "the doctrinal and liturgical uniformity of the Tudor ideal of Church government".[26] For Major, it was clear that despite the bloodiest of wars things could still get better. Although the stated aims of the Conference were somewhat ambitious, there was at the same time very little that was original or new in Major's introduction. Indeed, he followed in much the same direction as William Sanday before him, posing a question to his conservative opponents: "Will they accept the affirmation 'God was in Christ' with the practical recognition in daily life that 'Jesus is Lord' as constituting the irreducible minimum for modernist membership in the Church?"[27] For Major, as for the other contributors, Christ's divinity was certainly not open to debate but remained a doctrinal minimum.

The longer-term impact: Reshaping the Church of England

Even if the papers themselves were not as disturbing as was claimed by their more excitable opponents, what remains important is the longer-term effect they exercised on the Church of England. Most crucially, the Church's context had changed after the First World War, which meant that the term "liberal" was gradually transformed into the name of a party in the Church rather than just an adjective applied to some other party (like protestant or catholic or evangelical). What was perhaps most important about the Girton Conference was the part it played in the gradual mutation of what had hitherto been understood as simply the liberal or Modernist method of critical and doctrinal engagement into the name of a third Church party.[28] Rather than being another term

---

[26] Henry Major, "The Modern Churchmen's Conference of 1921", *Modern Churchman* 11 (1921), pp. 193–200, here at p. 200.

[27] Ibid.

[28] See Chapman, "Affirming Liberalism".

for the dominant ideology of the liberally educated Broad Church elite
of the Church of England, liberalism was transformed into a Church
party alongside the others.[29] The Girton Conference and its aftermath—
exemplified most crucially by the setting up of the Archbishops' Doctrine
Commission—played a crucial role in the development of the "three-
party" model of the Church of England, which continues to dominate
some Anglican identity myths.

The post-First World War period, however, was not a particularly
auspicious time for English liberal theology:[30] many of the most
influential German thinkers on English theologians before the First
World War—including for example William Sanday and F. C. Burkitt
(1864–1935) of Cambridge—were patriotic Germans such as Adolf von
Harnack, whose theological systems would forever be tainted for many
by their support of the German cause. At the same time, the wartime
alliances with Orthodox nations, especially Serbia and Russia, led to a
new interest in Eastern Orthodoxy, particularly from Anglo-Catholics
whose traditional anti-liberalism had been confirmed through the course
of the war.[31] Anglo-Catholicism had been further strengthened by the
remarkable success of the Anglo-Catholic Congress of June and July
1920, which meant it was moving away from its own self-identification
as a form of counter-cultural rebellion on the margins of the Church of
England with its own causes and campaigns over ritual or reservation

[29] Clive Pearson, "From Modernism to 'Majorism'", in Clive Pearson, Allan
Davidson and Peter Lineham (eds), *Scholarship and Fierce Sincerity: H. D.
Major the Face of Anglican Modernism* (Auckland, New Zealand: Polygraphia,
2006), pp. 47–71, here at p. 48.

[30] Mark D. Chapman, "The Evolution of Anglican Theology 1910–2000",
in Jeremy Morris (ed.), *Oxford History of Anglicanism: Global Western
Anglicanism* (Oxford: Oxford University Press, 2017), 5 vols, pp. iv, 25–49.

[31] See Mark D. Chapman, *Theology at War and Peace: English Theology and
Germany in the First World War* (London: Routledge, 2017), pp. 47–105;
and Mark D. Chapman and Bogdan Lubardic (eds), *Serbia and the Church of
England: The First World War and a New Ecumenism* (Palgrave Macmillan,
2022).

of the Blessed Sacrament[32] towards a far more mainstream force in the Church (as Major himself notes in some of his anti-Catholic asides in his introduction to the papers).[33] At the same time, Evangelicals were becoming increasingly anxious about policing boundaries, most obviously over permissible interpretations of Scripture and over the substitutionary atonement, but they tended to seek greater purity and isolation from others, including other Evangelicals with whom they disagreed (as is well illustrated by the split in the Church Missionary Society that led to the setting up of the Bible Churchmen's Missionary Society in 1922).[34]

It was into this increasingly partisan atmosphere that significant levels of self-government were introduced into the Church of England. The Church Assembly was established along with Parochial Church Councils in 1920 following the Enabling Act of 1919. Partisan identity was consequently strengthened in the early 1920s as the English Church was increasingly devolved from the state and became its own quasi-political organization with competing visions of theology and truth clamouring for control on the parliamentary model. As the Church adopted its own form of democracy, so it based its systems and structures on those of the English political system with its competing parties which had devolved the power to the Church in the first place. This meant that Gore and other campaigners were able to use the controversy following the Girton Conference to promote further partisan identity through efforts at forcing subscription to the Creeds by clergy, even if they proved unsuccessful. The invention of the Church Assembly made holding together the theological tensions and identities less a matter for the pragmatism of bishops and archdeacons and expanding diocesan administrations along with the cumbersome legal system, and more a matter for the institutionalized conflict of the Church Assembly, and

---

[32]   See John Shelton Reed, *Glorious Battle: The Cultural Politics of Victorian Anglo-Catholicism* (Nashville, TN: Vanderbilt University Press, 1996).

[33]   See Major, "The Modern Churchmen's Conference of 1921", p. 200.

[34]   Bebbington, *Evangelicalism in Modern Britain*, p. 218.

even (over certain matters including liturgy) in Parliament, as became apparent over the Prayer Book Crisis later in the decade.[35]

The "three-party" model of the Church of England

The "three-party" model of the Church of England was consolidated in the fallout of the Girton Conference and dominated the ways in which English theology developed in the 50 years or so afterwards.[36] This was noted in 1978 by Stephen Sykes, at the time Van Mildert Professor of Divinity at the University of Durham, in a slim and highly provocative volume entitled *The Integrity of Anglicanism*.[37] Sykes's book was intended as a piece of background reading for the Lambeth Conference of 1978 and offered a somewhat vigorous critique of Anglican comprehensiveness, which, he felt, had destroyed the coherence of Anglican theology and method in a messy compromise that could satisfy nobody. According to Sykes, the idolizing of a kind of theology that was based on partiality and fragmentariness rather than truth and consistency, to which even great theologians including F. D. Maurice and leaders such as Archbishop Michael Ramsey had succumbed, meant that there was an "exceedingly chaotic system of truth" at the heart of the Anglican Communion, and even more so in the Church of England.[38] Sykes was to explain things somewhat hyperbolically, even going as far as to make some rather strong accusations of institutional corruption:

---

[35] See Dan D. Cruickshank, *The Theology and Ecclesiology of the Prayer Book Crisis, 1906–1928* (London: Palgrave Macmillan, 2019).

[36] Mark D. Chapman, "The Fate of Anglican Liberalism", in Jörg Lauster, Ulrich Schmiedel and Peter Schüz (eds), *Liberale Theologie heute/Liberal Theology Today* (Tübingen: Mohr Siebeck, 2019), pp. 61–72.

[37] Stephen Sykes, *The Integrity of Anglicanism* (London: Mowbray, 1978). See Mark D. Chapman, *Anglican Theology* (London: T&T Clark, 2012), pp. 177–9.

[38] Sykes, *The Integrity*, p. 3.

there is something corrupt about an institution which presumes to mould the Christian allegiance of its millions of members and officially states that it bears testimony to the gospel of Christ, but which is unwilling or unable to face the issues of belief which are apparent to any informed Christian.[39]

Toleration of either diversity or comprehension, according to Sykes, had to be set against what he called "integrity", a virtue he finds to be almost entirely absent in his exposition of the Lambeth Conference resolutions and reports as well as those of the Church of England throughout the twentieth century. The bogeyman behind this incoherence, according to Sykes, was the excessively platonizing F. D. Maurice and his uncritical disciples such as Ramsey and Alec Vidler,[40] who were together responsible for the oft-repeated claim that there is no distinctively Anglican theology.[41]

In among Stephen Sykes's hyperbole there is a brief analysis of the Girton Conference in a chapter on "The Significance of Liberalism"[42] as perceived from the vantage point of the Church of England and the wider Anglican Communion of 1978. Sykes claims—accurately as I have shown—that the Modernists who were behind the Conference have had "an absurdly bad press"[43] and did not really set out to test the doctrinal limits of the Church of England and to see how far it could safely stray from Chalcedonian orthodoxy. Instead, he goes on, the position of most of the Conference's contributors was "only a minor regional variant of that of many German liberal protestants".[44] This is perhaps a rather less accurate statement since there was much lingering home-grown philosophical idealism among the contributors, but it is undoubtedly true of the more biblically focused papers. According to Sykes, the Girton lecturers were relatively orthodox churchmen who sought to challenge a few of the ways in which the Christian religion had been expressed in the

---

[39] Ibid., pp. 6–7.
[40] Ibid., p. 17.
[41] Ibid., p. 18.
[42] Ibid., pp. 26–35.
[43] Ibid., p. 27.
[44] Ibid., p. 27.

past by looking for an appropriate new language to express theological truths. Consequently, Sykes continues, "Far from hoping or intending to shock the orthodox in the wearisome manner of a group of middle-aged radicals, the modern churchmen had it in mind to provide an alternative to the rather bleak implications for Christology of some recent study by some fellow modernists, F. J. Foakes Jackson and K. Lake."[45] At the same time, however, Sykes also states that "no one has ever suggested that the modernist movement is really the core of the Church of England, in the way in which a generation of scholars have set out to canonise the liberal catholics".[46]

While Sykes's overall point and conclusion might be contested, what is important to note is the way in which what he regarded as a relatively insignificant group of liberal protestants was transformed into a Church party, even if he did not see them as particularly important. Indeed, for Sykes, far more important than what the Modernists said was the reaction to the Girton Conference and most crucially the setting up of the Doctrine Commission in 1923 to examine the boundaries of legitimate expressions of belief within the Church of England. It was this Commission that eventually led to a quasi-official recognition of a tripartite model of truth identified with each of the three parties. Initially the Commission was to have been chaired by Hubert Burge, Charles Gore's successor as Bishop of Oxford (and defender of the contributors to the Girton Conference against their opponents), but, following his death in 1925, the chairing was handed to William Temple, at the time Bishop of Manchester. The statement of the Commission's aims was published in *The Times* on 2 October 1925: the task was

> plainly a very big one, and the work is not of the sort that can be hurried, owing to the amount of preparatory labour that has to be done between the full sessions. Its discussions have dealt with the various kinds of authority for religious belief and with the doctrine of God, especially with the relation between justice and love in God, and with His relation to the world both

---

[45]   Ibid., p. 27.
[46]   Ibid., p. 26.

in miracle and otherwise. While it has not yet been possible to reach complete agreement, there has been a far greater approach to it than most people who know the widely divergent schools of thought represented would have anticipated. The Commission is encouraged to hope that its labours may enable it to help materially the growth of mutual understanding and closer agreement in the Church of England, partly by showing that views often regarded as divergent are in fact complementary, partly (when this proves impossible) by elucidating the precise points at which unresolved differences exist.[47]

The final report was certainly not hurried: it had to wait until 1938 for its publication. By that stage, Temple was Archbishop of York, and many things had changed both in the world and the Church of England: many of the theological challenges had obviously been reshaped by political and ecumenical developments.

The lengthy Report of the Commission is seen by Sykes as the finest example of what he calls the "crisis" (or incoherence) of the Anglican theology of comprehensiveness, especially the notion of the "complementarity" of truth[48] and the absence of any specific system of Anglican theology.[49] Indeed, Sykes highlights the introduction to the Report by William Temple which quite explicitly rules out the possibility of a specific system of "distinctively Anglican Theology" for "a systematic theology proceeds from premises regarded as assured", and this is impossible in the perpetual struggles of the Church of England. Instead, Temple goes on to claim that the Anglican Churches (and somewhat presumptuously he is using a Church of England report to speak for all the Anglican Churches):

---

47   *The Times* (2 October 1925), p. 15.

48   Sykes, *The Integrity*, p. 28.

49   Doctrine Commission, *Doctrine in the Church of England: The Report of the Commission on Christian Doctrine Appointed by the Archbishops of Canterbury and York in 1922* (London: SPCK, 1938), p. 25.

are heirs of the Reformation as well as of Catholic tradition; and
they hold together in a single fellowship of worship and witness
those whose chief attachment is to each of these, and also those
whose attitude to the distinctively Christian tradition is most
deeply affected by the tradition of free and liberal culture which
is historically the bequest of the Greek spirit and was recovered
for Western Europe at the Renaissance.[50]

Perhaps unsurprisingly, given his idealist background, Temple proposes
a synthesis between all three types of truth.[51] For Sykes, however, this
is a patent nonsense since he thought that a distinctive denominational
theological method based on a singular understanding of truth was
required for any church to be a church. That said, Sykes never quite
managed to pin down exactly what this method should be. His only
constructive proposal was a rather high doctrine of episcopal oversight
(which he was later to exercise as a bishop) along with invective against
those who did not think there was a distinctively Anglican method. At
least to those of a less dogmatic constitution, it may well be that Temple's
solution was rather more attractive than Sykes claimed: it certainly does
seem to me that the sort of humble and critical reformed Catholicism that
Temple identified is not necessarily a bad starting point for a coherent
theological method, even if it might be a little too uncertain for some
types of systematic theologian. Indeed, it may not be too bad a name for
an Anglican theological method that moves beyond the partisanship that
continues to infect the Church of England.

Conclusion

Sykes's more general point about the rise of a three-party model, however,
seems to be well made. Gore and others, somewhat unwittingly assisted
by Henry Major along with the ageing liberals of the Girton Conference,
managed to push liberalism into a box that made it mirror the historic

---

50   Ibid., p. 25.
51   Ibid., p. 26.

Church parties of catholic or evangelical. It is possible that the creation of a more partisan form of liberal theology helped marginalize the movement by removing it from the mainstream of Anglican theology, especially as this came to be dominated in the 1920s by Anglo-Catholicism in both its more liberal and conservative strands. The so-called Broad Church tradition, which had been the dominant theology of establishment Anglicanism (both high and low) through much of the nineteenth century, had consequently been transformed into a fairly modest group of "liberals" associated with the Modern Churchmen who, as with other parties, defined themselves in terms of what they were not as much as what they were. Just like the once great Liberal Party in politics, however, the liberal-minded Broad Churchmanship of the Anglican establishment as the dominant theological grouping, at least among the theology faculties and episcopal palaces, had begun to be supplanted after the First World War by a new force—a triumphalist Anglo-Catholicism—which for good or ill shaped the Church of England beyond all recognition. The good news for liberals, however, was that many Anglo-Catholics themselves came to adopt a strongly critical form of theology without succumbing to Henry Major's anti-ritualism. They often did the synthesizing that William Temple recommended but which proved increasingly difficult in a Church that had been divided into three. With the demise of Anglo-Catholicism and liberalism since the 1960s, however, the new dominant conservative ideologies in the Church of England seem to be rather less willing to establish a humble and critical reformed catholicism than were the Broad Churchmen or the liberal catholics of the past.

2

Imperial Theology and the Nicene Creed

Jonathan Clatworthy

The 1921 annual conference of the Churchmen's Union challenged elements of traditional Christian theology which had in fact been fourth-century innovations. The Nicene Creed was the product of a Roman imperial decision to turn Christianity into the cult of the political establishment. From being an egalitarian movement addressing the needs of the poor, the Church developed a theological justification for political oppression. Central to this change were the theological development of heavenly conflict between God, Jesus and the devil, the suppression of Jesus's humanity, and the imposition of centrally determined dogmas.

In 1921, Modern Church, then called the Churchmen's Union,[1] had been in existence for just over 20 years and had produced a substantial monthly journal for ten. They were far from convinced about some of the teachings Church of England clergy were expected to assent to, and called for open and honest discussion. Others were more determined to defend inherited teachings. Ordination was conditional on assenting to the Thirty-Nine Articles of Religion as laid down in the 1662 Book of Common Prayer.

My aim here is to illustrate how the elements of Church teaching that Modernists found most objectionable stemmed not from early Christianity but from the doctrinal changes of the fourth century. In a

---

[1]   The full title was The Churchmen's Union for the Advancement of Liberal Religious Thought.

nutshell, when the Roman Empire became Christian, Christianity had to become imperial.

To do this, I shall summarize the characteristics of imperial theology, how the Hebrew scriptures and early Christianity resisted it, and how the fourth-century changes overcame the resistance. I shall then return to the 1921 conference, noting how the doctrines that the Girton speakers challenged were the imperialist ones.

I shall draw on a range of disciplines. Before retirement, I alternated between being a parish priest and a university chaplain, and the contrast between the institutions intrigued me. Universities value new research—the newer the better, especially if it is *my* research. Churches value orthodoxy and tradition: the older the better, and don't you dare accuse me of innovating!

The gap keeps increasing, to the disadvantage of both. Churches need to catch up with research: sermons and official publications are often based on outdated theories. Academic research, meanwhile, is becoming more and more specialized, making it harder for scholars to relate to the bigger picture within which their research is located. Modern Church's role is, and was from the start, to illuminate the important theological questions by drawing fearlessly on the best scholarship.

The fourth-century setting

The theology of the fourth and fifth centuries changed the Church so successfully that today many Christians are unaware of the Christianity that preceded it.

By the early fourth century, city elites were used to public expectations that they would provide "good works", *euergetism*. Typically this involved occasional expenditures of large sums of money, either on a public building or on a festival offering entertainment and food. The beneficiaries were the citizens of the local city. In return, the donor would receive honour and status. However, every city also contained large numbers of destitute people who were excluded because they were not citizens. The only people who provided anything for them were the Christians.[2]

Constantine felt the need for an imperial cult that would unify the lands he controlled. He was not the first to do so, but by his day Christianity was the obvious candidate. Those city elites, therefore, if they wanted to advance their careers, started frequenting the churches. What they heard there was different. Many sermons from fourth-century bishops have survived, making far stronger demands. For example, Ambrose of Milan (339–97) could tell them:

> When you give to the poor, you give not of your own, but simply return what is his, for you have usurped that which is common and has been given for the common use of all. The land belongs to all, not to the rich; and yet those who are deprived of its use are many more than those who enjoy it. You are paying back, therefore, your debt; you are not giving gratuitously what you do not owe.[3]

Basil of Caesarea (329–79) argued:

> If one who takes the clothing off another is called a thief, why give any other name to one who can clothe the naked and refuses to do so? The bread that you withhold belongs to the poor; the cape that you hide in your chest belongs to the naked; the shoes rotting in your house belong to those who must go unshod.[4]

Oh dear. It was a common theme of Christian preaching. When John Chrysostom (c.347–407) told his congregation in the basilica of Antioch

---

2   Peter Brown, *Poverty and Leadership in the Later Roman Empire* (Hanover, NH and London: University Press of New England, 2002), pp. 4–10.

3   Ambrose, *On Naboth*, 53, quoted in Peter C. Phan, *Social Thought: Message of the Fathers of the Church #20* (Wilmington, DE: Michael Glazier, 1983), p. 163.

4   Basil of Caesarea, *Homily on "I will pull down my barns"*, 7, quoted in Phan, *Social Thought*, p. 117.

that "A woman must not walk past the poor with the price of many dinners hanging from her ears",[5] given the state of Antioch at the time we might wonder whether any of them had entered the basilica without walking past at least one beggar. It was a pointed challenge.

These sermons presupposed a different theology. The bishops saw wealth as given by God to provide for everybody; so whenever anyone went without, there was injustice. This was quite different from the pagan tradition. How did the difference arise?

Imperialist theology

Previously, hunter-gatherers had lived in small equal communities sharing their possessions. The lifestyle changed with the agricultural revolution. Wherever agriculture developed the surplus food was creamed off by the ruling classes and used to employ armies and tax collectors. Thus kings and emperors enriched themselves at the expense of their peasants. Ironically, and contrary to common modern beliefs about progress, the increased food supply led to more people going hungry.[6] Peter Garnsey summarizes this as follows:

> It used to be orthodoxy among anthropologists that the transition from hunter/gatherer to agricultural economies in prehistoric times enhanced the quality and stability of food supplies and

---

[5]   John Chrysostom, *In Matt.*, 89.4, quoted in Peter Brown, *The Body and Society: Men, Women and Sexual Renunciation in Early Christianity* (London: Faber and Faber, 1989), p. 312.

[6]   A major study was Gerhard E. Lenski, *Power and Privilege: A Theory of Social Stratification* (New York: McGraw-Hill, 1966). The implications for first-century Galilee are discussed by John Dominic Crossan, *The Historical Jesus: The Life of a Mediterranean Jewish Peasant* (San Francisco, CA: HarperCollins, 1992), pp. 43–6. See also Kent Flannery and Joyce Marcus, *The Creation of Inequality: How Our Prehistoric Ancestors Set the Stage for Monarchy, Slavery and Empire* (Cambridge, MA and London: Harvard University Press, 2012).

improved the health of the community, while reducing the
burden of labour on producers. More recently . . . the view has
gained ground that the adoption of sedentary farming, while
bringing "progress" in its train in the form of demographic
growth, cultural development and, in time, sophisticated
civilisations, also had undesirable consequences, namely, poorer
diets, lower nutritional status and greater vulnerability to famine
and malnutrition among ordinary members of the expanded
communities.[7]

Rulers offered theological justifications. Assyrian texts tell us that
Assur, the supreme god of Assyria, had become supreme by fighting
and defeating other gods. He was therefore rightly the god of the whole
world. As such he had established an order of nature and appointed the
king to maintain political order. An Assyrian myth distinguishes between
the creation of human beings, to relieve gods of toil, and the creation
of the king as a "human being who by virtue of his superiority makes
decisions".[8]

Just as Assur had fought and defeated other gods, the king's task was to
fight and defeat other kings.[9] To the peasant farmers—the overwhelming

---

[7] Peter Garnsey, *Food and Society in Classical Antiquity* (Cambridge:
Cambridge University Press, 1999), pp. 1–2.

[8] Eckart Otto, "Law and Ethics", in Sarah Iles Johnston, *Religions of the Ancient
World: A Guide* (Cambridge, MA and London: Harvard University Press,
2004), p. 87.

[9] "The king, as representative of the god Assur, represented order. Wherever
he was in control, there was peace, tranquility, and justice, and where he did
not rule there was chaos. The king's duty to bring order to the entire world
was the justification for military expansion. This idea pervaded royal rhetoric.
All that was foreign was hostile, and all foreigners were like non-human
creatures. Images of swamp-rats or bats, lonely, confused, and cowardly, were
commonly applied to those outside the king's control." See Marc Van De
Mieroop, *A History of the Ancient Near East* (Oxford: Blackwell, 2004), p.
243.

majority of the population—this meant high taxes and occasional visits by marauding armies helping themselves from their farms. The economic implications for human life were described accordingly. The best-known Mesopotamian texts are the *Atrahasis* and the *Enuma Elis*. Both describe how humans were created in order to relieve the gods of work, by maintaining temples and cooking their sacrificial meals. The *Enuma Elis* is also of interest because it was recited at Babylon's New Year festivals while the Jewish exiles from Jerusalem were there, in the sixth century BCE. Marduk, after becoming supreme by defeating other gods, declared:

> Blood I will mass and cause bones to be.
> I will establish a savage, "man" shall be his name.
> Truly, savage-man I will create.
> He shall be charged with the service of the gods
> that they may be at ease![10]

At this festival, a priest would lead the king to the temple of Marduk, remove his royal insignia and place them "before the god". He would then strike the king's cheek, accompany him to the presence of the god, drag him by the ears and make him bow down to the ground. The king would say "I did not sin." The priest would then console him, declaring that the god would exalt his kingship. It was an annual reaffirmation that the king's authority came from the god.[11]

We should not be misled by the modern idea that this was their *religion*. To use modern terminology, it was just as much their science and their economics: it explained why the world was the way it was. The gods had not designed us to be happy; they had made us to work. Poverty and suffering were only to be expected.

Within this theory every plague, flood, drought, and military defeat could be interpreted as punishment by the gods for inadequate sacrifices.

---

[10]   Ellen Van Wolde, *Stories of the Beginning: Genesis 1–11 and Other Creation Stories* (London: SCM Press, 1996), p. 193.

[11]   Walter Burkert, *Creation of the Sacred: Tracks of Biology in Early Religions* (Cambridge, MA: Harvard University Press, 1996), p. 96.

Each disaster implied the same moral: the sacrifices must be increased. In reality this was the main system of taxation. Justice was defined accordingly: it was about maintaining the power system and punishing people who resisted. Only the lucky few could expect a comfortable life. In these theologies we are hearing, of course, the voices of the rulers, who were the main beneficiaries.[12]

Characteristically, imperial theology presents itself as supreme and unchallenged, and thus more or less monotheistic, while at the same time defending its violence and oppression as a necessary response to real threats. Powerful humans, faced with evils and sufferings they have not overcome—and perhaps do not want to overcome—appeal to some other power or threat. In this way, as I have argued elsewhere, the quasi-monotheistic claims of imperial theology turn out to have a polytheistic foundation.[13]

The Hebrew alternative

Around the edges of those agricultural empires were societies more or less clinging onto the older, more egalitarian values. One such text has survived, offering an alternative account of why humans were created: the Hebrew scriptures known to Christians as the Old Testament.

The first chapter of Genesis reads like an emphatic rejoinder to the *Enuma Elis*. We do not know that it was, but it seems most unlikely that its authors were unaware of the Babylonian text. By comparing the two, we can see what the authors of Genesis 1 were claiming. The one and only God needs nothing from us but has created humans and other living beings as a free gift, to bless us for our own sakes. The text asserts that

---

[12] For a description of Mesopotamian sacrifices, see Karen Rhea Nemet-Nejat, *Daily Life in Ancient Mesopotamia* (Westport, CT and London: Greenwood Press, 1998), pp. 178–95.

[13] J. Clatworthy, *Why Progressives Need God: An Ethical Defence of Monotheism* (Winchester: Christian Alternative, 2017), Chapter 1.

the created order is good both in the sense of benefit and in the sense of moral good.[14] Imperialist values appear elsewhere in the Bible, but that is another story. As an account of the human condition Genesis 1 could hardly be a greater contrast with imperialist theology. Instead of constant pressure of work, there is a balance between work, rest, and celebration. Justice is not about maintaining the hierarchy: instead it is about making sure everybody benefits from the blessing.[15] Even the story of the Flood is turned on its head, so that instead of being a punishment for inadequate sacrifices it becomes a guarantee of a secure environment.[16]

Sometime later, editors decided that this first chapter of Genesis would make a good preface to their other scriptures: laws commanding kings to protect the poor; prophets condemning kings for not upholding the laws; and histories attributing the loss of national independence to the failures of the kings.[17]

---

[14]   Mark Smith, *The Priestly Vision of Genesis 1* (Minneapolis, MN: Fortress Press, 2010), writes: "Creation is good in both meanings as benefit and moral good. Within the priestly worldview, both aspects of 'good' fall under the rubric of holiness. God is good in all these respects, and when God creates, creation is likewise good.", p. 62.

[15]   The tension between these two accounts of justice is still with us. John Rawls's influential *A Theory of Justice* (Oxford: Oxford University Press, 1972) defends relative equality on the basis of his thought experiment of a "veil of ignorance"—in effect a God's-eye-view—though Rawls did not describe it this way. Many of his opponents, beginning with Robert Nozick, *Anarchy, State and Utopia* (Oxford: Blackwell, 1974), saw justice as a matter of adhering to contracts.

[16]   Genesis 6–9; Claus Westermann, *Genesis 1–11* (Minneapolis, MN: Fortress Press, 1994), pp. 393–406.

[17]   Rainer Albertz, *A History of Israelite Religion in the Old Testament Period, Vol. 1: From the Beginnings to the End of the Exile* (London: SCM Press, 1994), pp. 489–90.

The early Christian Church

By the time of the Roman Empire, therefore, there was a well-established Jewish egalitarian tradition, expressed in their scriptures but in conflict with normal practice. How did the early Christians relate to it?

There is ample literary evidence of Christian concern for the destitute from the fourth century onwards. It has been argued that this was because poverty was increasing then.[18] However, this is a minority view. Alternatively (or additionally), poverty was already well established, but we hear about it more from the fourth century onwards because it could be more publicly addressed once emperors were supporting the Church. Much depends on how high destitution levels were.

On this question there has been much scholarly debate. At one extreme, Greek and Latin literature mention episodic famines[19] but not long-term malnutrition and hunger. This may be because only a minority were literate. Just as the majority of journalists today show little interest in the continuing rise of dependence on food banks, nearly all Roman imperial literature was written by and for the elite.

At the other extreme, some anthropologists and sociologists, drawing on comparative studies, have argued that in agricultural empires like Rome around 90 per cent of the population would have been at, below, or close to starvation level.[20] Recent examinations of skeletal remains provide further information.

Opinions vary,[21] though Peter Garnsey's detailed studies suggest that most of the population had enough to eat much of the time but were constantly threatened with shortage.[22] There was more money in the

---

[18] E. Patlagean, *Pauvreté économique et pauvreté sociale à Byzance, 4e–7e siècles* (Berlin: De Gruyter Mouton, 1977).

[19] Michael Ivanovitch Rostovtzeff, *The Social and Economic History of the Roman Empire* (Oxford: Clarendon, 1957), especially pp. 599–601.

[20] A classic text is Lenski, *Power and Privilege*.

[21] A range of views is expressed in E. Margaret Atkins and Robin Osborne (eds), *Poverty in the Ancient World* (Cambridge: Cambridge University Press, 2006).

[22] Garnsey, *Food and Society*, pp. 2 and 43–60.

cities than in rural areas, so it was realistic for St Paul to urge the Church at Corinth to "put aside and save whatever extra you earn"[23] to help the Jerusalem Church where there was real destitution.

Pagan literature does provide evidence of beggars. This seems to imply that people gave to them, but on this point there is very little literary evidence. The traditional line on beggars was that they should be ignored; any giving should be to citizens who could offer something in return. Stoics advised against feeling pity, whether or not one gave. The poor were considered more likely than the rich to feel pity for beggars, as a product of fear for themselves.[24] The elder Seneca cited the orator Blandus saying that a woman would give to a beggar especially if she had exposed a child. Handing over the money, she would think "perhaps this is my son".[25] John Chrysostom reported that poor parents were blinding their own children to make beggars of them.[26] Another reason for giving would have been to shake off an importunate beggar. Several ancient sources comment on Cynics abusing those who refused to give.[27] As the evidence is sparse, we should not make too much of it, but clearly these reasons for giving are a far cry from the bishops' reasons cited above.

Given this situation, how did the first Christians address it? For a long time, twentieth-century scholars showed little interest in the historical Jesus. Since the 1970s, however, there has been a great deal of new research.[28] Much of it responds to the findings about contemporary social

---

23 1 Corinthians 16:2.

24 Anneliese Parkin, "You do him no service", in E. M. Atkins and R. Osborne, *Poverty in the Ancient World*, pp. 64–5.

25 *Controversiae* 10.4.20, quoted in Parkin, "You do him no service", p. 72.

26 John Chrysostom, *In I Corinth.* 21:5, quoted in Parkin, "You do him no service", p. 72.

27 Parkin, "You do him no service", p. 74.

28 This is known as the "Third Quest for the Historical Jesus". The "First Quest" was led by nineteenth-century Germans, until Weiss and Schweitzer argued that Jesus had mistakenly foretold an imminent end to the age. There was then a gap. Not only did a mistaken preacher seem not worth studying, but also levels of antisemitism were high, and it could not be denied that Jesus was a Jew. Scholarly interest was revived in the "Second Quest" of the middle

conditions. A characteristic theme has been to understand Jesus's teaching on the Kingdom of God as a revival of the egalitarian themes in the Jewish tradition and its application at a time of widespread starvation in Galilee. From an imperial perspective Galilee was a remote backwater, useful as a source of taxation but not much else. When the taxes demanded were not forthcoming, soldiers would move in and burn the villages down. Anyone they captured would be sold on the slave markets. Those who escaped would have little alternative but to run to the wilderness and join a group of bandits. Debt and food, the practical concerns at the centre of the Lord's Prayer, were the dominant issues not just of Galilean families but of whole communities. Many Jesus scholars locate Jesus's teaching about the Kingdom of God within this context.[29]

Richard Horsley, for example, argues that Jesus went round the villages urging the people to renew the covenant with God described in Exodus 20, Deuteronomy 5 and Joshua 24. He takes Luke 6:20-2 and 11:2-4 to have originated with a covenant renewal speech.[30] Deuteronomy 15:1 commands the cancellation of all debts every seven years. If they were to do that, and concentrate on making sure everybody got something to eat,

---

of the twentieth century. The "Third Quest" is often seen as beginning with Geza Vermes's *Jesus the Jew* (London: Collins, 1973). Since then Jews and Christians have collaborated on the research, drawing on a wide range of sources—classical, anthropological, sociological, and archaeological.

[29]   John Dominic Crossan, *The Historical Jesus*; Elisabeth Schüssler Fiorenza, *In Memory of Her: A Feminist Theological Reconstruction of Christian Origins* (London: SCM, 2nd edn, 1995); Richard A. Horsley, *Jesus and the Politics of Roman Palestine* (Columbia, SC: University of South Carolina Press, 2013); Douglas E. Oakman, *Jesus and the Peasants* (Eugene, OR: Cascade, 2008) and *Jesus, Debt, and the Lord's Prayer* (Eugene, OR: Cascade, Wipf and Stock, 2014); Bruce Longenecker and Kelly Liebengood, *Engaging Economics: New Testament Scenarios and Early Christian Reception* (Grand Rapids, MI: Eerdmans, 2009); Luzia Sutter Rehmann, *Rage in the Belly: Hunger in the New Testament* (Eugene, OR: Cascade, 2021).

[30]   Horsley, *Jesus and the Politics of Roman Palestine*, pp. 44–5.

the community would stand a better chance of surviving. I have argued elsewhere that this was the origin of the Eucharist.[31]

Two texts in the book of Acts tells us that the early Church maintained it:

> All who believed were together and had all things in common; they would sell their possessions and goods and distribute the proceeds to all, as any had need.[32]
>
> Now the whole group of those who believed were of one heart and soul, and no one claimed private ownership of any possessions, but everything they owned was held in common. With great power the apostles gave their testimony to the resurrection of the Lord Jesus, and great grace was upon them all. There was not a needy person among them, for as many as owned lands or houses sold them and brought the proceeds of what was sold. They laid it at the apostles' feet, and it was distributed to each as any had need.[33]

If Luke was not mistakenly idealizing the early Church this was a radical development, drawing on the Hebrew scriptures to cope with an extreme situation. It must have worked well, as a kind of village-based food insurance policy. Thereafter, it seems to have expanded and been applied in other social settings. Many subsequent Christian writers appealed, in some way or other, to the principle that wealth has been given by God to provide for everyone, so any surplus should be given to those in need: we can cite the *Didache*, Justin Martyr, Clement of Alexandria, Tertullian, Origen, Cyprian, Lactantius, Basil of Caesarea, Gregory of Nazianzus, John Chrysostom, Ambrose, Augustine and Gregory the Great. It is a long list. Earlier texts described what the churches were doing. Later ones, from the fourth century onwards—like the ones cited above—addressed

---

[31]   J. Clatworthy, "Hunger and the Origins of the Eucharist", *Modern Believing* 61:3 (2020), pp. 239–50.

[32]   Acts 2:44–5.

[33]   Acts 4:32–5.

wealthy people and told them it was their Christian duty to give to the poor.[34]

In addition to these texts, from Constantine's time onwards we get occasional glimpses from elsewhere. There is a report from the city of Ancyra that

> what is wont to happen in all great cities occurred here too: for in the porticoes of the church there was gathered a crowd of people, some unwed, others married, lying there for their daily food. It happened one time in winter that a woman was lying in labor in the church portico at midnight.[35]

A party of travelling monks is reported to have visited the Egyptian town of Oxyrhynchus on a Saturday night. They found the church porch occupied by poor people awaiting the Sunday distribution of food. One of the monks reported:

> And as we lay down, there was a poor man with a single mat, half of it lay beneath him and half was pulled over him. It was bitterly cold. Getting up to pass water, I heard him groaning with the pain of the cold, but comforting himself, saying "Thanks be to Thee, Lord, how many rich men there are at this time who are in prison, some bearing chains, others with their feet in the stocks, not even able to get up to pass water. And here I am, free as the Emperor himself, to stretch both my legs".[36]

There is a fifth-century account of St Lawrence, a third-century martyr. Lawrence was a deacon of the Church at Rome, and as such responsible for the church's finances. According to the story the Prefect commanded him to hand over the wealth of the church. He obeyed it like this:

---

[34]   For a list of citations see Phan, *Social Thought*, 1984.

[35]   Palladius, *Historia Lausiaca*, quoted in Brown, *Poverty and Leadership*, p. 12.

[36]   F. Nau, "Histoires des solitaires égyptiens", no. 214, *Revue de l'Orient chrétien* 13, p. 282, quoted in Brown, *Poverty and Leadership*, p. 12.

He runs about the city gathering into one flock the companies
of the infirm and all the beggars who cry out for alms . . . There
a man showing two eyeless sockets directs his straying, faltering
footsteps with a stick; a cripple with a broken knee; a one-legged
man . . . Here is one whose limbs are covered with running sores
. . . Such people he seeks out through all the public squares, used
as they were to being fed by Mother Church . . . There stood the
company of poor men in their swarms, a ragged sight. They greet
the Prefect with a roar for alms.[37]

We have no way to check the accuracy of the story, but it would have
made no sense unless the Church was widely known as the main source
of support for beggars.

Constantine

We have seen how the bishops cited above said the rich *owed* their surplus
wealth to the poor as a matter of justice, because wealth is created by God
for this purpose. Feeding the hungry was a product of their theology.

As emperor, however, Constantine continued to wage wars, grab booty,
and lavish it on his favourites, just as his predecessors had done and his
successors would continue to do. From his perspective, Christianity had
another weakness. As an empire-unifying cult, it was too diverse. Bishops
spent their time arguing against each other. Constantine instructed them
to produce an agreed statement of faith so that he could then establish
it as the empire's cult.

Before Nicaea, some New Testament epistles had contained brief
credal statements. Candidates for baptism had learned off by heart
summaries of the faith which varied from place to place. At Nicaea, what
the bishops agreed, under imperial pressure, was a string of propositions
that could command majority support. The Council innovated in two

---

[37]   Peter Brown, *Through the Eye of a Needle: Wealth, the Fall of Rome, and the
Making of Christianity in the West 350–550* AD (Princeton, NJ: Princeton
University Press, 2013), pp. 77–8.

ways: by using imperial power to enforce its decisions and by defining orthodoxy,[38] thus establishing the dogmatic principle that all Christians ought to believe the same things. "This is what we believe" became "this is what we have to believe". Ever since then Christians have lived with that tension between an enquiring mind and the obligation to believe what they are told.

Not that the Council stopped the arguing. Basil's brother, Gregory of Nyssa (c.335–c.395), described the culture of their age thus:

> If you ask about your change, the shopkeeper talks theology to you, on the Begotten and the Unbegotten; if you inquire the price of a loaf, the reply is: "The Father is greater and the Son is inferior"; and if you say "Is the bath ready?" the attendant affirms that the Son is of nothing.[39]

For a century and a quarter, from 325 at Nicaea to 451 at Chalcedon, bishops gathered at councils and defined the Church's teachings in keeping with the emperor's wishes. It is sometimes claimed that the disagreements had finally been resolved by Chalcedon; more realistically, after Chalcedon it had become too difficult for bishops to do so much travelling. The conflicts between Orthodoxy, Monophysitism and Nestorianism were finally resolved not by Chalcedon but, centuries later, by Islam.[40]

---

[38]   So argues Frances Young in *The Making of the Creeds* (London: SCM, 1991), especially p. 13.

[39]   Peter Brown, *Power and Persuasion in Late Antiquity: Towards a Christian Empire* (Madison, WI: University of Wisconsin Press, 1992), pp. 89–90.

[40]   Diarmaid MacCulloch, *A History of Christianity* (London: Penguin, 2010), Chapters 7 and 8.

The Nicene Creed

Constantine, just like his Assyrian and Babylonian predecessors, wanted a theology that approved of both military conquest and economic exploitation. Suffering, therefore, had to be due either to divine punishment of sin or to transcendent forces outside imperial control. The Nicene Creed provides accordingly. Most of it is about Christ, from being eternally begotten to his future coming in glory. In the middle we are briefly told about his appearance on earth:

> For us and for our salvation he came down from heaven: by the power of the Holy Spirit he became incarnate from the Virgin Mary, and was made man. For our sake he was crucified under Pontius Pilate; he suffered death and was buried.[41]

We are given not the slightest inkling of what Jesus said and did that made people call him the Messiah or the Son of God.

It was "for our salvation". In the Hebrew scriptures, the two great moments of salvation were escape from Egypt, with the giving of the Law at Sinai, and return from exile under the Persian settlement. In the New Testament, the Greek word for salvation, *sōtēría*, is also the word for welfare, prosperity, healing, deliverance, and preservation. Its cognate, *sōtēr*, means "saviour", "deliverer" or "preserver".[42] Imperial theology, however, needed to disconnect salvation from this earthly life—since there was no intention to improve the lot of the majority—and transfer it to the next. Theologians could not deny that Jesus had been crucified by Roman authority, or that crucifixion was reserved for enemies of the state, with the result that they rewrote the story, borrowing pagan themes. From then on, the crucifixion of Jesus was to be all about negotiations in heaven. For over half a millennium, until at least Anselm's time at the end of the eleventh century, the dominant account of what Jesus achieved

---

[41]   Church House Publishing, *Common Worship: Services and Prayers for the Church of England* (London: Church House Publishing, 2000), p. 234.

[42]   S. G. Green, *Greek Testament Vocabulary and Synonyms* (London: Religious Tract Society, 1905), p. 514.

was the Victory Theory of the Atonement. Just as earlier Assyrian and Babylonian emperors had justified their warmongering by appeal to warmongering gods, fourth-century Christians began to justify imperial rule by appeal to heavenly conflict between the Father and the devil, involving death by the Son.[43]

But in that case, how did the devil ever get so much power in the first place? A backstory was needed to explain it. Although Genesis does not say so, Christian interpretation took the serpent in the Garden of Eden to be the devil in disguise, tempting Eve and Adam contrary to God's intentions.[44] But these theories were not new. Polytheistic cults abounded with stories of how one god had created the world and others had messed it up. Before Constantine, Christianity had been a diverse movement with different groups borrowing or repudiating different pagan theories. What was new with Nicaea was that the doctrines of heavenly salvation and the Fall were established as normative for Christian belief. Christians searched their scriptures for texts which could be interpreted this way.[45]

Thus fourth-century Christianity recreated the imperial theology characteristic of large empires. Christian emperors could now see themselves as representing Christ the *Pantocrator*: the ruler of all. Earlier, when Jesus had been described by Mark and Matthew as the King of the Jews,[46] by Luke as the saviour of Israel,[47] and by John as the saviour of the world,[48] their intention had been defiance: Jesus is a better king than Herod, a better saviour than Augustus. Their first readers would have understood this. After Constantine, though, Christ the Pantocrator became the divine *endorsement* of the world's Herods and Augustuses. The last person an emperor would ever want to represent

---

[43]   J. N. D. Kelly, *Early Christian Doctrines*, 5th edn (London: A&C Black, 1968), Chapter 14; Gustaf Aulén, *Christus Victor: An Historical Study of the Three Main Types of the Idea of the Atonement* (London: SPCK, 1950).

[44]   Kelly, *Early Christian Doctrines*, Chapter 13.

[45]   The closest texts are Romans 5:12–14 and 8:18–23.

[46]   Mark 15:26; Matthew 2:1–2.

[47]   Luke 1:68–9; 24:21.

[48]   John 4:42.

was a community activist from a peasant village who had been executed as an enemy of the state.

In case there was any doubt about the obligation for Christians to believe what they were told, the Creed's final sentence made it clear. It was subsequently removed, but as agreed at Nicaea it ran:

> But as for those who say, There was a time when He was not, and Before being born He was not, and that He came into existence out of nothing, or who assert that the Son of God is from a different hypostasis or substance, or is created, or is subject to alteration or change—these the Catholic Church anathematizes.[49]

Today hardly anyone cares, let alone anathematizes anyone. Then, it mattered. As the empire became Christian, Christianity had to borrow the clothes of pagan philosophy which knew how to please emperors. Douglas Oakman writes that over time the memory of Christians

> suppressed knowledge of Jesus's historical praxis, which in the eyes of the Roman Order led justly to the cross, and replaced that political memory with the dramatic story of Jesus's incarnation, his emptying or *kenōsis*, and after humiliation his exaltation to have his own eternal kingdom. Ironically, this eternal kingdom came to serve the needs of centralized agrarian power and taxation, so that the Constantinian Order of the era of the Nicene and Constantinopolitan Creeds would in one important respect betray the memory of Jesus.[50]

Sermons like those of Ambrose and Basil, common though they were for a while, were not going to last. Sooner or later emperors would make sure the bishops were more to their liking. Anti-imperial versions of Christianity survived in the monasteries and various movements denounced as heretical. In the sixteenth century, people who disagreed with what they were told to believe were called atheists; in the eighteenth

---

[49]   Kelly, *Early Christian Doctrines*, p. 232.
[50]   Oakman, *Jesus, Debt,* p. 6.

they were called deists. Many histories have written those dissidents out of the story of Christianity as though they had not been Christians at all; but this is to prejudge the issue.[51]

The 1921 conference

There always were dissidents, impressed by Jesus but not by imperial theology. The 1921 Conference on "Christ and the Creeds" stood in this tradition. The remainder of this chapter describes its contribution.

The Churchmen's Union was founded at the end of the nineteenth century. Atheism had been advancing, its proponents claiming that science was on their side. In response many churches, both Catholic and Protestant, reaffirmed older dogmas. The word "dogma" itself, originally from a Greek word meaning "opinion", had by the end of the nineteenth century been turned into a concept valued by Catholics and Protestants alike: a divinely revealed truth, proclaimed as such by Church teaching, and binding on the faithful.[52]

Liberals were less fearful. To resist atheism, they aimed to offer educated critics a version of Christianity consistent with modern knowledge. Although the British Empire was at its height and Modernists presented little opposition to it, the dogmas they challenged at this conference were characteristic of imperial theology: specifically, the suppression of Jesus's humanity and the obligation to assent to credal dogmas.

They were accused of denying the divinity of Christ. They rejected the accusation, but in a manner which critics found unsatisfactory. Henry Major's editorial review of the Conference summarized what was at stake:

[51] Dominic Erdozain, *The Soul of Doubt: The Religious Roots of Unbelief from Luther to Marx* (Oxford: Oxford University Press, 2016); Alec Ryrie, *Unbelievers: An Emotional History of Doubt* (London: William Collins, 2019).

[52] Alan Richardson and John Bowden (eds), *A New Dictionary of Christian Theology* (London: SCM, 1983), art. "Dogma".

The question discussed was this: What is the relation of the
Divine Nature to the Human Nature in Jesus, and what do we
mean precisely when we ascribe Divinity to Jesus? The leaders
of the Conference were agreed in their answer that the Deity of
Jesus is to be seen in His perfect Humanity.[53]

Hastings Rashdall's analysis was the most thorough, and characteristic
of liberal opinion at the time. Rashdall argued that Christ

had not merely a human body, but a human soul, intellect, will.
This was not always recognized by the Church. Many of the
earlier Greek fathers—Irenaeus, for instance, and Athanasius—
obviously thought of Him simply as the Logos of God residing
in a human body. Later councils condemned this position in
the person of Apollinarius . . . And I fear a great many people
who now think themselves particularly orthodox are really
Apollinarians too.[54]

If the human Jesus was in any sense divine, there must be a real common
characteristic between humanity and divinity:

If "divine" and "human" are thought of as mutually exclusive
terms, if God is thought of as simply the Maker of man, if
man is thought of as merely a machine or an animal having no
community of nature with the universal Spirit who is the cause
or source or "ground" of the existence alike of Nature and of
other spirits, then indeed it would be absurd to maintain that
one human being, and one only was both God and man at the
same time.[55]

But in that case, what is the connection? *How* was he divine? To Rashdall,
if this is to be possible at all there must be "a certain community of nature

---

53   *Modern Churchman*, September 1921, p. 196.
54   *Modern Churchman*, September 1921, p. 279.
55   *Modern Churchman*, September 1921, p. 281.

between God and man", so that "in the highest ideals which the human conscience recognizes there is a revelation of the ideal eternally present in the Divine Mind".[56] Jesus was different in degree, not in kind, from the rest of us:

> If we believe that every human soul reveals, reproduces, incarnates God *to some extent*; if we believe that in the great ethical teachers of mankind, the great religious personalities, the founders, the reformers of religions, the heroes, the prophets, the saints, God is more fully revealed than in other men ... then it becomes possible to believe that in one Man the self-revelation of God has been signal, supreme, unique.[57]

Thus the divinity of Jesus was to be understood in a spiritual and moral sense: he expressed the divine in a human life that set an example for others to follow. This position contrasts with those who preferred a more distant Christ—not so much an example for Christians to follow, more a heavenly agent working on our behalf, as expressed in the Nicene Creed and the Victory and Substitution theories of the Atonement.

The difference between the two perspectives is familiar to anthropologists of religion. Pre-Axial indigenous spiritualities characteristically have a two-stage account of time. In the first, the world order was created. This was sacred time. Thereafter, they expect life to carry on without any significant change. Events and activities become meaningful to the extent that they express, or in some way re-enact, what happened in that sacred past.[58]

This account of time contrasts with the sense of continuing historical change that modern society has inherited from Axial Age movements like

---

[56] *Modern Churchman*, September 1921, pp. 281–2.

[57] *Modern Churchman*, September 1921, p. 283. Empirically, of course, we do not have enough evidence to know whether Jesus lived a life more morally perfect than anyone else; but that was not debated. What got people steamed up was the stress on Jesus being fully human just like other people.

[58] Mircea Eliade, *A History of Religious Ideas* (Chicago, IL: University of Chicago Press, 1978), Chapter 11.

the ancient Hebrew prophets. In one worldview, no significant changes are expected. The important work has already been done, so what we do does not matter so much. In the other worldview, there is a stronger ethical component, since human actions affect what the future will be like.

Although modern society is dominated by this latter worldview, reversions to the other can often be observed. The imperial theology described above has all the hallmarks of it: Creation, Fall and Redemption in Christ, though spread out over time, constitute the world order conceived to be fundamentally unchanging from the Resurrection to the Second Coming.

So: was Jesus a divine computer engineer who came to earth to install a new motherboard for the world, and then left us to get on with life as before? Or was he a human so full of God that he showed us how we too can be full of God? The Modernists of the 1920s, keen to engage with new insights from scientific, historical, and literary studies, naturally supported the progressive theory. For all that Rashdall claimed to be defending the divinity of Christ, what he meant by it was not what his opponents believed.

As for the Creeds, in the 1920s public opinion was on the side of the Modernists. Contemporary understandings of history and evolution could not be reconciled with them. Cyril Emmet, one of the Conference speakers, argued:

> Historical Christianity has seemed to imply a view of the world, its origin, its fall, the method of its redemption, a view of the relation between God and man, between Heaven and earth, which is to many untenable in an age of evolution with its wider conception of the universe. There must be a thoroughgoing restatement of religious beliefs, such as will harmonize with the new outlook.[59]

---

[59]   Cyril Emmet, "The Modernist Movement in the Church of England", *The Journal of Religion* II:6 (1922), p. 575.

The Girton speakers were not against Creeds altogether, but thought they should be minimized and only recited on special occasions. On this matter, Harold Anson's paper is the most interesting. Anson responded to a question by the Unitarian James Martineau. Martineau had asked:

> How can you Anglicans sleep at nights when for all you know your baker may be confounding the Persons, and your butcher may divide the Substance?

Anson replied:

> As a matter of fact the baker and butcher, if their fancy led them to sing tenor and bass in the choir, would cheerfully chant the whole Confession of Faith without one qualm of conscience, while we should be excluding all those who feel that the philosophical statement of a creed is in itself so difficult that it never ought to be made a test of fellowship, or of office.

The wrong people are excluded:

> By our modern creed, we find that people are excluded because they doubt the Virgin Birth; but who could imagine our Lord saying to any man who wished to follow Him, 'Let me first hear what you believe about my mother.'

He still wanted a Creed:

> Still you . . . want a creed which . . . will make the butcher and the baker tremble, the butcher when he sells bad meat, and the baker when he overcharges for his bread.[60]

Underlying the debates lay the question of how one seeks truth. Emmet summarized the position of liberals:

---

[60]   All quotations from Anson are from *Modern Churchman*, September 1921, p. 333.

> Modernism is not primarily the acceptance of a set of opinions and new dogmas, critical or scientific. Any given Modernist may or may not believe in the Virgin Birth, or the empty tomb, or the apostolic authorship of the Fourth Gospel. The essence of Modernism lies, not in its conclusions, but, in the way they are reached and the temper in which they are held.[61]

Thus, liberals were content to keep questions open rather than expecting to establish the right answer for all time. The questions were to be asked for their own sakes, not as a technique for enforcing uniformity or distinguishing true Christians from others.

In these Conference papers, therefore, we can observe a tension which has echoed throughout Christian history. Should we accept, as settled for all time, the doctrines inherited from the Church's past, or is there a proper role for questioning them and seeking new truths? Does our understanding of Christ tell us that the nature of human experience is determined by the interactions of heavenly beings, or does it tell us that we, following Jesus, can make a difference to what life is like in the future?

Imperial theology, like most forms of polytheism, explains the good and bad features of human experience in terms of interactions in the divine realm. Life is to be accepted as it is, with all its tragic elements. The explanations are treated as permanent truths; the possibility of a better alternative is denied.

To oppose imperial theology, at the very least one needs to believe that the human mind is capable of judging inherited beliefs. The speakers at Girton believed it was. The debate illustrates a tension which is as old as history. The Hebrew scholar John Barton has explored the role of natural theology in the development of Old Testament laws. He notes a characteristic process. The earliest texts associated with a particular law often indicate a specific reason for it. Later texts, like for example summarizing conclusions to a whole set of laws, more often describe them as simply given by God. The implication is that new laws were introduced for specific purposes, but when they had been in force for

---

[61]   Cyril Emmet, "The Modernist Movement", pp. 562–3.

some time—or when a reactionary movement reintroduced old laws—
the original reasons were often replaced by simple appeals to God's will.[62]

On reading the debate about the 1921 conference, one finds a similar
pattern. The opponents of the Girton Conference offered few rational
arguments. Their responses included precious little systematic theological
defence of Christ's divinity or the accuracy of the Creeds. There was no
echo of the early Church's debates. What stirred up the emotions, rather,
was the very idea of questioning traditional teachings.

On this matter the Churchmen's Union was adamant. To Henry Major,
the Modernist was opposed to the exaltation of the ability to profess belief
in dogmas into a Christian virtue of a high order.[63] E. O. Iredell argued:

> There is a fear of Truth itself, expressed today in the cautious and
> specious admission that theological enquiry should be allowed
> *within certain limits*. Who has any right to prescribe such limits
> save God? What have we to fear from the frankest investigation?
> If the Creeds are true, there can be no objection to free and
> unlimited discussion of them. If they are not true, then the sooner
> they are unmasked and disposed of the better for all of us.[64]

A century later, in the light of what we find credible today, it is worth
asking: did the defenders of the traditional doctrines, a hundred years
ago, save Christianity? Or did the questioners point the way to a more
authentic pre-imperial interpretation of the man from Nazareth?

---

[62]   John Barton, *Ethics and the Old Testament* (London: SCM Press, 1998),
       Chapter 4.
[63]   Henry Major, *English Modernism: Its Origin, Methods, Aims* (Cambridge,
       MA: Harvard University Press, 1927), p. 79.
[64]   *Modern Churchman*, 11:9 (1922), p. 466.

3

Does it matter if Jesus did not think of himself as divine?

Alan Race

This chapter gives full weight to the impact of the rise of historical consciousness and critical thinking in Christological discourse. The main impact has been to set in train the full recovery and affirmation of the humanity of Jesus through Jesus of History research and a frank reckoning with the changing fortunes of the reception history of the historical figure through the centuries. This, in turn, leads to a revision of what it means to imagine Jesus as "Saviour", and the proposal to interpret him in the language of "symbol" and "parable" is explored.

The impact of historical consciousness

Historical enquiry is an irritant for most systematic theologians. In the area of Christian thought labelled Christology, it might too easily lead to the kind of startling conclusion exhibited by New Testament and Jesus-scholar, Gregory C. Jenks:

> As a historian, I see no reason to impute to Jesus any personal awareness of divinity or messianic identity. As a Christian, I have no need for a Christ figure whose authentic humanity is

> compromised by the Christology that has become normative for
> later generations of Christians.[1]

This kind of assessment is startling for at least two reasons. First, traditionally the divine self-awareness of Jesus was accepted as part and parcel of the affirmation of him as a divine–human figure sent by God for the salvation of the world, but very few New Testament historians now consider such self-awareness to be a decently grounded assumption about him. Second, the accusation that the later normative doctrine of Jesus as God incarnate compromised his human identity strikes close at the heart of Christian faith itself, in spite of the in-principle acknowledgement of Jesus's human nature in the Christological two-nature divine–human formulation from the Council of Chalcedon (451 CE). Of course, while it was never wholly possible to ignore the human identity of Jesus, throughout Christian history it has nevertheless been seriously underplayed, leading to the comment by the theologian Donald Baillie, in his book *God Was In Christ*,[2] that the Church has operated through the ages with a form of hidden Docetism, the view that the humanity of Jesus was a pretence at humanness, the real operative principle being the divinity of the saviour himself.

In Christological debate, it was alleged that we do not need to know about Jesus *historically* because that has no bearing *philosophically* on the problem of how the human and divine natures of Jesus might cohere in the one person. We just needed to know that he did display a certain humanness as part of his divine–human make-up. Still, it was necessary that that humanness was grounded in some appeal to history, however minimal—for example, in the self-consciousness of Jesus, that he knew himself to be, as in John's Gospel, "one with the Father". However, this is an appeal that is no longer open to us: these words are an interpretation

---

[1]   Gregory C. Jenks, "The Once and Future Jesus", in Gregory C. Jenks (ed.), *Historical Afterlives of Jesus: Jesus in Global Perspective 1* (Eugene, OR: Cascade Books, 2023), p. 18. My essay here is sympathetic to these remarks by Gregory Jenks.

[2]   D. M. Baillie, *God Was In Christ* (London: Faber and Faber, 1956; first published by New York: Scribner, 1948).

by the Johannine Church and are unlikely to stem from Jesus himself. No wonder systematicians are irritated by historians! Perhaps the fact that history yields uncertain results is just what we have to live with. As it is, G. E. Lessing's (1729–81) dictum that "Accidental truths of history can never become the proof of necessary truths of reason" seems applicable.[3] Today it is no longer possible to downplay the humanity of Jesus. The impact of historical consciousness and awareness of cultural change has made sure of that, and liberation, feminist, anti-racist and post-colonial theologies have exploited it further. However, there are consequences of this insistence on paying more than lip-service to the humanity of Jesus, and this has been challengingly expressed by the New Testament scholar and colleague of Gregory Jenks, John Dominic Crossan:

> Christianity must repeatedly, generation after generation, make its best historical judgment about who Jesus was then and, on that basis, decide what that reconstruction means as Christ now.[4]

That's the kind of remark that has the systematicians reaching for the smelling salts! But at least it has the advantage of reclaiming the full humanity of Jesus and his impact on the stage of history.

Crossan's remark seeks the maximum continuity between Jesus in first-century Palestine and Jesus thereafter as interpreted through the Christian imagination. If there's something to attend to here, it means that we first have to have a view on what Jesus stood for: an outline of his teachings and deeds, his place in the cultural setting of his own times, and the scope and purpose of his overall impact through early

---

[3]   G. E. Lessing, "On the Proof of the Spirit and of Power", in Henry Chadwick, *Lessing's Theological Writings: Selections in translation with an Introductory Essay by Henry Chadwick* (London: Adam & Charles Black, 1956), p. 53. Original German, 1777. A similar assessment was also made by Graham Shaw, *The Cost of Authority* (London: SCM Press, 1983), p. 274: "[h]istorical method is intrinsically hostile to claims of metaphysical uniqueness."

[4]   John Dominic Crossan, *Jesus: A Revolutionary Biography* (New York: HarperSanFrancisco, 1994), p. 200.

Christian texts. Then, hard on the heels of any resulting picture, the hermeneutical enquiry into how that resulting picture resonates with, applies to, and challenges the cultural contexts of contemporary diverse societies, including interreligious contexts, follows.

The task of reconstruction is daunting of course, for Jesus-scholars make very different estimates of Jesus at the historical level. Still, the daunting apart, there is precedent for different estimates of Jesus in the fact that the four Gospels are themselves four different assessments of the Jesus figure, each bringing to bear their own assumptions, circumstances, and experiences in the portraits they have shaped and bequeathed to us.[5]

Two bookends

So what might we say historically? Let me cite two Christian writers—two bookends, as it were, standing at either end of the twentieth century—one from 1906 and one from 1995. The first is the famous quotation from the polymathic Albert Schweitzer (1875–1965) coming at the end of his magisterial *The Quest for the Historical Jesus*:

> He comes to us as One unknown, without a name, as of old, by the lake-side, he came to those men who knew Him not. He speaks to us the same word: "Follow thou me!" and sets us to the tasks that He has to fulfil for our time. He commands. And to those who obey, whether they be wise or simple, He will reveal Himself in the toils, the conflicts, the sufferings that they shall pass through in his fellowship, and, as an ineffable mystery, they shall learn in their own experience Who He is.[6]

---

[5]   For the purposes of the historical study of Jesus, I leave aside the witness of Paul the Apostle who pays scant attention to the historical figure of Jesus.

[6]   Albert Schweitzer, *The Quest of the Historical Jesus: A Critical Study of Its Progress from Reimarus to Wrede*, tr. William Montgomery (London: Adam & Charles Black, 1910), p. 403; original German, 1906.

Magnificent words, even if a little opaque for our times. For how does "ineffable mystery" square with what Jesus's followers learn "in their own experience"? Schweitzer thought that Jesus, through his execution, wanted to force the apocalyptic Kingdom of God into history, for judgement and hope. That Jesus failed in this does not matter; for his words and actions, based in transcendent power, have the potential to unsettle every age after him and open people's eyes to the reality of what God has to offer in their own struggles and sufferings. At least, this appears to be Schweitzer's view.

Now set this alongside the following citation from Marcus Borg (1942–2015)—Jesus-scholar and former colleague of Crossan—with words spoken on NBC Radio in the United States on Good Friday 1995:

> Jesus was from the peasant class. Clearly, he was brilliant. His use
> of language was remarkable and poetic, filled with images and
> stories. He had a metaphoric mind. He was not an ascetic, but
> world-affirming, with a zest for life. There was a socio-political
> passion to him—like a Gandhi or a Martin Luther King, he
> challenged the domination system of his day. He was a religious
> ecstatic, a Jewish mystic, for whom God was an experiential
> reality. As such, Jesus was also a healer. And there seems to have
> been a spiritual presence around him, like that reported of St.
> Francis or the present Dalai Lama. And as a figure of history,
> Jesus was an ambiguous figure—you could experience him and
> conclude that he was insane, as his family did, or that he was
> simply eccentric or that he was a dangerous threat—or you could
> conclude that he was filled with the Spirit of God.[7]

So at one end of the century we have Jesus the apocalyptic preacher and at the other end we have Jesus the wisdom teacher, one whose sharp words jolted people out of complacency, who introduced people to the compassionate yearning of God for a world remade (healed), who set himself decisively against the domination system of Roman rule, and

---

[7]   Marcus Borg, *Jesus: Uncovering the Life, Teachings, and Relevance of a Religious Revolutionary* (New York: HarperSanFrancisco, 2006), p. 164.

who thought that God's kingdom could be entered into in his present because it was a kingdom for the transformation of God's world now and extending into the future.

How to choose between Schweitzer and Borg? Marcus Borg thought that roughly the Jesus scholarship world was divided 50:50 between the two broad outlines: 50 per cent think Jesus was an apocalyptic preacher and 50 per cent a mystic wisdom teacher. Most of us might feel lacking in competence to make a choice! Part of the reason why the discrepancy exists is to do with what has happened in the intervening period between 1906 and 1995. Here I point briefly to four factors influencing the shift in perspectives through the century:

- First, we have become more used to the recognition that the New Testament texts themselves are church-shaped and author-shaped books. Jesus speaks the theological language of the author of the Gospel. He is made to answer the questions, challenges, and issues of later times when the Gospels were published in the final quarter of the first century.

- Second, we have learned more about the social world of first-century Palestine than we knew previously: a world of social, political, and economic oppression, of vested interests and brutality, of Jews who would not tolerate the Roman transformation of land into commodity because the land ultimately belonged to no human being but to the Almighty alone.

- Third, we have learned to emphasize the Jewishness of Jesus. It is probably this factor more than any other that places a question mark against whether or not Jesus thought of himself as divine. But it also places Jesus on a spectrum of Jewish voices in the circumstances of his time—even some of his radical sayings can often be found to be part and parcel of Jewish sources if we dig deep enough.

- Finally, we have had a period in the twentieth century of the deepening of critical consciousness and its effects on theological construction. So we have become less enamoured of miracles as part of an argument for the divinity of Jesus; we are less sure about seeing inside the self-consciousness of Jesus for a clue to his messiahship; and we can be frank about the strangeness in cultural worldviews between the first and later centuries and our own.

To go straight to the heart of Christian orthodoxy in the language of incarnation, accumulations in critical consciousness uncover why lines of development happened, but they also alert us to the fact that most of the building blocks for orthodox belief in incarnation are just not part of what counts as theological reasoning now, and we can't alter that fact. For example, what does it mean for us to assent to the pre-existence of Jesus, a cornerstone assertion in the formation of classical Christology? These observations have led one Dutch writer to say that the definition of the Council of Chalcedon (451 CE)—that Jesus was human and divine in one person—is simply "a phase in reception history, albeit one which lasted a long time and left deep traces",[8] but can exercise no claim to be the benchmark of Christianity for all time. Obviously, these shifts in context strike at the heart of inherited Christian identity. Moreover, the claim that Chalcedon was "a phase in reception history" should alert us to the observation that there have been many phases in reception history, something that has been illustrated in numerous books.[9]

---

[8]   H. M. Kuitert, *Jesus: The Legacy of Christianity* (London: SCM Press, 1998), p. 129.

[9]   Chris Keith, et al. (eds), *The Reception of Jesus in the First Three Centuries*, 3 vols (London: T&T Clark, 2020), provides a detailed account of what is entailed in the processes of "reception history".

The Pelikan test

One such book is by Jaroslav Pelikan in his masterly survey, *Jesus Through the Centuries: His Place in the History of Culture*.[10] Jaroslav has 18 chapters, roughly corresponding to 18 centuries. These can be tabulated as follows, and I have added two further instances of my own, thereby updating the total reception history to 20.

1. The Rabbi	2. The Turning Point of History	3. The Light of the Gentiles	4. The King of Kings
5. The Cosmic Christ	6. The Son of Man	7. The True Image	8. Christ Crucified
9. The Monk Who Rules the World	10. The Bridegroom of the Soul	11. The Divine and Human Model	12. The Universal Human
13. The Mirror of the Eternal	14. The Prince of Peace	15. The Teacher of Common Sense	16. The Poet of the Spirit
17. The Liberator	18. The Man who Belongs to the World	19. Feminist Jesus Black Jesus Post-Colonial Jesus	20. Interfaith Jesus

Let me illustrate the point about reception history by highlighting just three of Pelikan's portraits: the Cosmic Christ; the Monk Who Rules the World; the Universal Human. This will be sufficient to illustrate how Jesus has taken on some very different personas down the ages. I

---

[10]   Jaroslav Pelikan, *Jesus Through the Centuries: His Place in the History of Culture* (New Haven, CT and London: Yale University Press, 1985).

shall illustrate the portrayals through Christian art, mostly supplied by illustrations in Pelikan's book.

The Cosmic Christ

Traditio legis, Sarcophagus of Junius Bassus.[11]
359 CE, marble (Treasury of St Peter's Basilica)

It is astonishing how Jesus came to occupy this position as the one who rules the cosmos. His rise over three centuries from Galilean peasant preacher and healer to ruler of the highest proportions over the cosmos is breathtaking. Much of this has to do with the promotion of Christianity as the official religion of the empire under the Roman Emperor Constantine. Converts to the faith (whether real or instrumental) included the elites of Roman society, such as Junius Bassus (*d.*359) whose sarcophagus, shown here, carries this image of Christ as cosmic ruler. Junius had converted to Christianity shortly before his death, but during his life he was responsible for the administration of the city of Rome.

---

[11] Source: <https://commons.wikimedia.org/wiki/File:Sarcophagus_of_Junius_Bassus.jpg>. Photo: Matthias Kabel (CC BY-SA).

In terms of art, the figure of Jesus supplants the usual depiction in Roman art of the emperor as ruler of everything earthly, that is, under the heavens. In the sarcophagus relief, Jesus places his feet above and below the dividing line between the heavens and the earth depicted as a curved arc over the head of *Caelus*, the personified ruler of the cosmos and symbol of Roman authority. In other words, the status of Jesus is greater even than that of the Roman emperor. Jesus rules over the heavens and the earth.

Intellectually, the "exaltation" of Jesus to be ruler of heaven and earth owes much to the role of the *logos* idea in ancient Greek philosophy. The *logos* assumed the role of mediator between Hebrew and Greek understanding, as has been explained clearly by the historian and Jesus-scholar, David Galston:

> To some degree, the Jewish Bible gave to early Christians the Word of God, but almost immediately the Greek Logos defined what the Hebrew Word should mean. "Christ" stopped meaning the "Anointed One" (*christos*) and started to mean the "Word" (*logos*), and the Word was the begotten of God who carried two natures. In the Bible the Word is the spirit of God given to the prophets; in rising Christianity the Word is the universal reason of God embedded in the cosmos and incarnate in Christ.[12]

The question for us from this remains two-fold: first, what do we make of that slippage in language between Hebrew and Greek?; and, second, what sense can we make of the personification of the *logos* idea, stemming from a wholly bygone world—to a large degree alien to us, irrespective of how much we lay claim to comprehend the terms of its use—and its adoption by Christian understanding as the meaning of Jesus for all time? My own answers are: (i) slippage between languages nearly always alters meaning, and (ii) the personification of *logos* sets in train a misleading

---

12   David Galston, "Jesus as the Logos: The Afterlife of Jesus in Ancient Philosophy", in Gregory C. Jenks (ed.), *Historical Afterlives of Jesus: Jesus in Global Perspective 1* (Eugene, OR: Cascade Books, Wipf & Stock, 2023), pp. 92–109, here at p. 93.

application of the term and leads to the imponderable problem of having to affirm the pre-existence of Jesus.

The Monk Who Rules the World

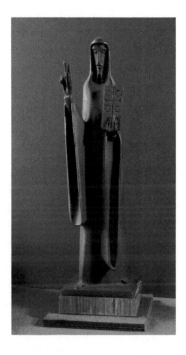

With this portrayal of Jesus, we move from high politics and high philosophy to renunciation of both, shifting the focus more towards a spirituality filter. The image accompanying this iteration of Jesus in Pelikan's book is a statue entitled *Pax Christi*.[13] Here Jesus rules the world by renouncing it! This is Jesus as radical critic, confronting the world's pretences to status, power, and wealth. The monk denies worldly self-aggrandisement by reclaiming the Gospel saying of Jesus, "If anyone would come after me, let him deny himself and take up his cross and follow me" (Mark 8:34). The contrast between Jesus as cosmic ruler and as renunciation ruler could not be greater. Yet clearly both are intended

---

[13]   Photo by Alan Reed, OSB. Used by permission of Saint John's Abbey, Collegeville, MN.

as interpretations of the historical Jesus figure. The *Pax Christi* depiction has Jesus dressed in the clothing of a Benedictine monk and is highly stylized, holding the scriptures in one hand and blessing with the other. Pelikan comments on the symbolism by noting that "the monks began by patterning themselves after Christ. But by the time they were finished they were likewise patterning Christ after themselves."[14] There may be at least one leading advantage in the monk representation, however, and that is that it reclaims a sense of Jesus as human being, albeit one whose renunciation in ideal terms excels that of his follower monks. We are in the realm of spirituality and not theology or politics.

The Universal Man (Human)

In some respects, it is possible to believe that the depiction of Jesus as monk is a precursor of later developments, in so far as the humanity of the saviour was beginning to be embraced. However, we can safely say that the embrace of the humanity of Jesus comes into its own with the

---

14   Pelikan, *Jesus Through the Centuries*, p. 110.

dawn of the renaissance period in European history. The renaissance, viewed through Christian art, with its emphases on individualism and human subjectivity, was not so much a retreat from Christian faith into what came to be known as Humanism, as a fuller acknowledgement of what the classical belief about Christ—that he was divine *and human*—promised. The illustration that Jaroslav chooses for this development is the image of *The Saviour* by El Greco (Kyriakos Theotokopoulos), painted in about 1610. The portrayal stands somewhere between the older icon style of Christian art and the later more fully realist style. The result is a "transfigured Christ", a fully human being yet transfused with divine light placed not only behind the head of Jesus but evident throughout his whole body. It is what has been called the "divinely human" Christ, depicting the destiny of our humanness as a form of Christlikeness. We are not meant to see Jesus here as "only human" but feel the full impact of traditional incarnation doctrine communicated through the subtlety of light suffusing his form as human being. Pelikan cites Erasmus (1467?–1536) as clinching what El Greco would later paint: "When you abandon the world for Christ, you do not give up anything. Rather, you exchange it for something far better. You change silver into gold, and rocks into precious gems."[15]

On this view, Christian salvation does not remove a person from the world but completes the human potential, raising fallen humanity to heights not possible without the embodiment of it in the human Christ. Christ the transfigured human signifies our human purpose. It is a view that would surface again at the Girton College Conference on "Christ and the Creeds" in 1921, as indicated in the chapter by Jonathan Clatworthy in this volume (p. 56): "the divinity of Jesus is his fulfilled human life".

My own preferences illustrating this divinely human view are presented in two other paintings from the renaissance period—*The (Adolescent) Saviour* by Leonardo da Vinci/Giovanni Antonio Boltraffio (1490–5) and *Self Portrait* by Albrecht Dürer (1500)—paintings not reproduced in Pelikan's book.

---

[15] Pelikan, *Jesus Through the Centuries*, p. 156.

The (Adolescent) Saviour[16]   *Self Portrait*[17]

Da Vinci's *Saviour* (there is some doubt over da Vinci's origination) depicts Jesus through and through as the embodiment of beauty, youthfulness, androgyny—and also vulnerability. God is not the aged immoveable rock of ages, but the vulnerable lover who dwells within the vulnerable human.

For Albrecht Dürer's *Self Portrait*, if ever there was a statement about the total fusion between the divine and human this would be it. The measure of our humanness lies in the humanness of the Saviour. One might call this theological fusion. Its artistic form repeats the theological affirmation that salvation celebrates the realization that it is "Not I, but Christ who lives in me".

Pelikan has taught us that Jesus really has meant different things to different Christian people through the ages. Yet his tabulated depictions raise a troubling question for the scholars of Christology. Are these

16   <https://commons.wikimedia.org/wiki/File:Giovanni_Antonio_ Boltraffio_-_The_Adolescent_Saviour_-_Google_Art_Project.jpg>, accessed 8 December 2023.

17   <https://en.wikipedia.org/wiki/Self-Portrait_(D%C3%BCrer,_Madrid)#/ media/File:Selbstportr%C3%A4t,_by_Albrecht_D%C3%BCrer,_from_ Prado_in_Google_Earth.jpg>, accessed 8 December 2023.

depictions simply illustrations of the accusation that those who search for the human Jesus simply end up with an idealized reflection of themselves? This is the well-known accusation of the nineteenth-century Catholic theologian, George Tyrrell, commenting on the search for Jesus by the liberal Protestant, Adolf von Harnack: "The Christ that Harnack sees, looking back through nineteen centuries of Catholic darkness, is only the reflection of a Liberal Protestant face, seen at the bottom of a deep well."[18] Tyrrell's accusation could be aimed not only at nineteenth-century "historical Jesus" research but also at the whole of Christian history as Pelikan has shown. Whether we are talking of Jesus as *pantocrator*, or as the monk who rules the world, or as the divinely human fulfilment of human being, the projection of any era's values and ideals on to the portrait of Jesus, at least to a degree, on the one hand seems unavoidable. On the other hand, representation of Jesus reflecting terms of different cultural embodiments seems necessary if Jesus is to mean anything to—connect with—a particular culture at a particular time. It may be possible to avoid the "peril of modernizing Jesus"[19] while simultaneously combining this with the risk of depicting Jesus in terms which address the needs and aspirations intrinsic to any cultural grouping and people. This is the challenge at the heart of Christology for a historically conscious age. Perhaps it may be possible—though it would be a stretch—to claim that the varying images of Jesus through the ages reflect some element in the enduring appeal of Jesus's personal character, thereby providing a warrant for whatever an image is intended to convey. But demonstrating this historically would seem virtually impossible.

We are left with the question of what to make of the afterlives tapestry of Jesus. What it conveys, first of all, is that the classical Christological question—"How can God become human?"—under conditions of historical consciousness, cultural contextuality, and stress on humanness has been reconfigured, even reversed. It seems to me that Crossan's Christological challenge aims to negotiate the pitfalls in as realistic and

---

18   George Tyrrell, *Christianity at the Cross-Roads* (Eugene, OR: Wipf & Stock, 2006), p. 49; first published by Longmans, Green and Co., 1910.

19   Henry J. Cadbury, *The Peril of Modernizing Jesus* (Eugene, OR: Wipf & Stock, 2006; first published by Macmillan, 1937).

theologically sensitive a manner as possible: "Christianity must repeatedly, generation after generation, make its best historical judgment about who Jesus was then and, on that basis, decide what that reconstruction means as Christ now."[20] Facing that challenge, we have no other option in our reflection on Jesus and his impact than to begin with the broad strokes of what we might know about the Jesus figure historically and from that estimation, which is always provisional, enquire into how it is that such a figure is exalted to the status of being revelatory. This I what I wish to pursue in the next section of this chapter.

Gospel interpretations

We begin with the New Testament and have to face candidly the fact that it does not supply us with a biography of Jesus in the normal sense of that genre. What we know of him is filtered through the symbolic responses from the first Christian communities. For all of the New Testament writers, Jesus is characterized as God's agent who brings transformation/ salvation by fulfilling the prophecies of the ancient Hebrew scriptures, who acts on God's behalf in order to transform the human condition, personally and politically, in order to establish the whole world as the arena of God's hope and work for justice and compassion. The "whole world" of course referred to the tiny portion of the world that was known to those writers at the time.

New Testament writers vary over how they depict this impact of Jesus, some being almost wholly conceptual in their approach (for example, Paul and the writer to the Hebrews), and others using more of a story-narrative style (for example, the Gospel writers). As the cultural framework and theological worldview informing these portrayals are largely alien for twenty-first-century human beings (in spite of any familiarity we may suppose that we have with them), we therefore have to make a huge act of historical imagination to appreciate what is being communicated through them.

---

[20] See above p. 63.

Let me now supply some familiar pen portraits. Paul, the first Christian writer we know, said virtually nothing about Jesus at the historical level, but he thought of Jesus as the agent of God at the end of the present age for drawing both Jews and Gentiles into the new age in Christ. He explained God's action by applying to Jesus a number of images and terms, all present in his Jewish background, which picked up on the sense of divine agency. They included, for example, the term "son of God", which echoed the important role that Jewish thought at the time gave to significant figures in Jewish life—"sons of God" could be used of kings of Israel, angels, holy exemplars of faithfulness, even Israel as a whole. But as Paul applied it to Jesus, he was *the* son, the one through whom all people could find their relationship with God as adopted sons and daughters. We should not equate Paul's use of this term with what the later tradition made of it in Christian doctrine—God the Son, the second person of the Trinity existing in heaven before coming to earth as a divine–human being. Other titles that Paul employed, such as second Adam, Saviour, Messiah, and Lord, function in a similar way, each picking up a Jewish term or symbol and seeing Jesus as bringing its potential sense to a head. We should add also that some of those interpretations of Jesus were essentially anti-Roman—not *that emperor* but *this peasant teacher* is Lord, Saviour, and bringer of peace etc. These were staggering claims and assertions.

The Gospels are different. While resembling historical narratives, they are in fact imbued with the theological integrity of each writer as a whole. For Mark, the earliest Gospel writer, Jesus is depicted as a healer/exorcist, a deeply mysterious, angular challenging figure, who disturbs religious complacency and confronts the wilful obduracy of everyone who would stand in the way of the announcement of the Kingdom of God. He is the "son of man", a suffering figure who accepts the inevitability of his brutal execution by the state as the climax of his vocation. He dies totally abandoned and the reader is left to work out his or her own response to the upheaval which Jesus has unleashed. For Matthew, Jesus is a teacher of a new and more stringent divine law. As Moses had brought the law down from a mountain, so Jesus, the new Moses, teaches the new law from the top of a mountain—the "sermon on the mount"—in all probability itself a Matthean creation. For Luke, Jesus is the ideal model of human compassion, the moral exemplar given for all to emulate. The idealism reaches untold proportions, for example in the forgiveness that Jesus pronounces, even as the nails are driven into his hands on the cross—"Father forgive them for they know not what they do". When it comes to John's Gospel, at the end of the first century, the symbolic significance of Jesus takes a different turn. Jesus becomes, more abstractly and mythologically, the "Word" or the "Wisdom" of God, the one beside God at the dawn of creation, bringing order out of chaos. In a famous verse, Jesus is said to reveal God's mind: he is the "word made flesh", the very clue to the creative purposes of God.

These thumbnail sketches all endow Jesus with symbolic significance according to the particular perceived meaning they give to the reality of the transformation/salvation which Jesus is said to bring. So: Jesus brings a victory over sin, death, and Roman oppressive power, at the end of the age (Paul); confronts social and political evil and wilful human stubbornness with the present and future Kingdom (Mark); provides new, demanding teaching (Matthew); sets the exemplary standard for the moral life (Luke); and reveals the mind of God (John). These sketches are the result of treating the literature as being indicative of creative minds and they move beyond the older concentration on titles alone given to Jesus.

Once this varied picture of early responses to Jesus is accepted it becomes notoriously difficult to know with any accuracy exactly what Jesus said and did, but a number of features are bound to be present in most portraits. Let me simply list them:

1. Jesus preached the coming Kingdom of God—whether that was in the near apocalyptic future or to be entered into in the present. The content of the Kingdom, though not always clear, involved both personal transformation and non-violent resistance to the massively exploitative domination system of Rome. Preaching the Kingdom puts Jesus in line with the Hebrew prophets and singles him out as a radical critic of the abuse of power.
2. His experience of the sacred places him in the category of Jewish mystic. He was someone who lived out of his own centredness in the divine reality.

3. He healed and performed exorcisms. This too must have been a persuasive part of his attraction: healing stories centred on him form a strong impression in all early traditions. (How we understand exorcism in the present is a separate and intriguing question.)

4. He made stringent demands about the narrow way, such as the summons to leave family and security; and he taught what was involved in the compassion of God. This puts him in line with other Jewish wisdom teachers.

5. He had a circle of 12 close followers and preached probably mostly to Jewish people. This makes him a movement initiator. It may be that Jesus not only entertained a vision of the Kingdom of God but also had a programme to bring it about. This could well have been built around healing and shared eating, both potentially subversive activities when measured against the social conventions of the Roman world.

6. In championing the cause of the Kingdom of God he died a martyr for his cause, as confrontation with the powers of oppression was inevitable, whether Jesus himself sought martyrdom or not.

Now, while none of these factors are beyond dispute, and perhaps more could be added, they all have a sufficient grounding in New Testament traditions that they give a minimal picture of the so-called "Jesus of history". The New Testament scholar, Leslie Houlden, sums it up as follows:

> [W]ithin and behind the diverse ways of expressing the experience derived from Jesus, the New Testament witnesses to certain dominant trends, worked out with various thoroughness and direction. All found through him a new vision of God. It meant a new sense of urgency of God's call and the immediacy of his power, a new awareness of gracious acceptance by him and solidarity with those of like mind, with a hitherto unfound

freedom to give primacy to love, itself seen with new clarity to be rooted in God himself.[21]

And he draws the conclusion, radical for some: "Whether it is just or useful to give to such a conviction the name 'incarnation' may be disputed."[22]

My view here accepts the validity of that conclusion. From a historical point of view, we are dealing with a figure whose impact was such that he brought about a transformed outlook which was total, and it seems clear that as a result he achieved a speedy and all-embracing symbolic significance. It is a significance that arose initially from the interaction between the particular cultural and religious conditions of Jewish and Roman life at the time, on the one hand, and his own impact as a figure on the stage of history bearing the characteristics we have surmised, on the other hand. Moreover, this is how it has always been: religious need, social conditions, intellectual outlook, historical memory—all factors which are never static—combining to produce any era's estimate of Jesus's revelatory power.

Jesus—Transforming parable

The effect of the historical approach to our subject is that it gives us a glimpse behind the scenes to see the factors at work in any Christian assessment of Jesus. It is too wooden simply to say that the Christian view of Jesus is that he is the Messiah or Son of God or whatever other title was applied to him, in some ahistorical sense. Glimpsing behind the scenes leaves us with a combination of factors which form the building blocks for any assessment of who Jesus is for Christians at any one period in history. These can be specified as follows:

1. the theological worldview in which his followers are set

---

[21] J. L. Houlden, *Patterns of Faith: A Study in the Relationship Between the New Testament and Christian Doctrine* (London: SCM Press, 1977), p. 55.

[22] Ibid.

2. the outline of him which comes through the grid of the New Testament
3. the transformation/salvation he is believed to enact.

These factors are all variable, depending on the historical circumstances, and they have been at work continuously through Christian history. This brings me to my constructive proposal for the remainder of this chapter.

For theologians who want to give due weight to the realities of cultural change, what shape can reflections about the theological or Christological value of Jesus take? My own response is to show how the three factors involved in any account of Jesus combine to form what I call the transforming parable-view of Jesus.

Becoming a transforming parable is akin to other forms of how persons achieve symbolic significance as heroes or role models. Think of how Gandhi achieved significance as a symbolic focus of hope at a time of immense cultural change, combining intellectual and political skills with religious practice in the struggle for India's independence from British colonial rule. Extending this process to the religious sphere, religious communities and cultures are bound to invest certain key figures with symbolic significance in a scope which is all-embracing. This is what I am suggesting happened to Jesus of Nazareth.

To approach our subject through a consideration of how persons achieve symbolic or parabolic significance has not been the usual Christian route for reflecting on the figure of Jesus. Yet there are pressures in our culture, deriving from historical, humanistic, and psychological modes of thought, which press us towards this approach. Such an approach has at least the value of not turning Jesus into a philosophical problem or puzzle. Whatever he stood for, he made an impact at the human level, and we are left responding to that impact even 2,000 years later.

Therefore, let me turn in conclusion to the three factors in my estimate of Jesus as transforming parable, and flesh them out further.

First, in relation to a theological worldview. My inclination is to locate the transcendence of God immanently in the midst of historical and human affairs. We do not look to God to intervene in human affairs from outside of our experience, but we know God in the midst of life as part of human experience. In this sense, as some theologians put it, God is always incarnating Godself; or, to use alternative but still traditional language: the activity or presence of God in creation and salvation is a single divine action. Precisely how the relationship between divine and human initiatives is construed in this (and in any) theological account remains an intriguing and challenging problem, but it entails that there is no difference in principle between that relationship of grace with human response in us and in the figure of Jesus.

Second, Jesus can be said to stand within the continuum of divine–human relationship as a powerful instance of what it is to live unconditionally in the presence of God. To cite the New Testament scholar, E. P. Sanders: Jesus "thought that he had been especially commissioned to speak for God, and this conviction was based on a feeling of personal intimacy with the deity".[23] Or, similarly, Marcus Borg:

> Jesus stands in this tradition of Jewish figures for whom God, the sacred, was an experiential reality. The data in the Gospels supporting this claim are early and widespread ... They are found in the earliest layers of the gospel tradition ... Texts report visions, long hours of prayer, and a sense of the presence of the Spirit in him. His language often expresses an intimacy with God ... More generally, his wisdom teaching often reflects a transformed perspective and perception most compatible with an enlightenment experience of the sacred. His passion and courage as a prophet suggest an experiential grounding in God like that of the prophets of the Jewish Bible.[24]

These are more or less agreed citations from two authors—Sanders and Borg—who disagreed on many other aspects of historical Jesus research.

Now, if these estimates are correct, it does provide some historical backing for the symbolic value of Jesus as a transforming parable. To interpret his life in this manner entails that he both represents the offer

---

[23]   E. P. Sanders, *The Historical Figure of Jesus* (London: Allen Lane, Penguin Press, 1993), p. 239.

[24]   Borg, *Jesus*, p. 117.

of God's presence to the world and also becomes a route for our human response to that presence, and, as it were, activates it. In that sense, he remains a mediatorial figure. He both enacts the purposes of God in word and deed, initially in one particular setting and culture, and also sharpens our human responses—through the symbolic power which he embodies and releases—to those same divine purposes in different cultural settings thereafter. This is how parables, as enacted symbols, work: they mediate. It is what I believe those two images of Da Vinci and Dürer were seeking to convey: Jesus does not stand apart from the human, but through his impact and legacy activates the drive towards transcendence in all of us.

This interpretation is close to that of the Jesuit theologian, Roger Haight, whose impressively comprehensive book, *Jesus: Symbol of God*, argues that the language of incarnation is essentially a function of the concept of revelation. Through his humanity Jesus renders present the infinite reality of the transcendent God, and in the process activates our human response to that same reality, for the sake of the transformation of the world. As Haight has expressed it: "On his part, Jesus of Nazareth, the human being, pointed to something other than himself, namely God and God's rule in history. And on the part of the interpreter, one approaches him with the religious question, looking for salvation that comes from beyond, from God."[25] Symbols integrate both objective and subjective factors in the religious response to life's quest for meaning and purpose: Jesus offers the presence of God, but that in turn is mediated only in terms of our subjective receptivity, which is varied in terms of our human needs, questions and yearnings. Hence the varied portrayals of Jesus in the New Testament and through the centuries.

My third factor in the case for how Jesus is a transforming parable considers the meaning of transformation/salvation today. Transformation/Salvation, I take it, has to do primarily with liberation from the forces which kill the spirit of life, and these embrace both private and political dimensions of our humanity. The political forces, including ecological impact, might have material-sounding names, such as poverty, exploitation, oppression, and fear for the very possibility of

---

[25] Roger Haight, S. J., *Jesus: Symbol of God* (Maryknoll, NY: Orbis Press, 1999), p. 203.

human survival; or they might have other more psychological-sounding names, unfortunately familiar in our culture, such as despair, loneliness, meaninglessness. Transformation/Salvation is not a rescue operation, but a preparedness to take responsibility, in partnership with God, for the future of life on earth.

These concerns may seem removed from both the New Testament and the early classical centuries, but we have to be honest in recognizing the cultural distance between then and now. Nevertheless, it is possible to root some of these concerns in the impressions that we have of the impact of Jesus himself. For example, the stories of his inclusion of the poor and outcast; the reversal of values that his message of the Kingdom of God entailed; his compassion for human beings who fail; his seeming disregard for rigidity when it comes to practical religious ethics; and his confrontation with the collusive religio-imperial oppressive powers of empire. The first century of the Christian era may have cherished vastly different assumptions and values in life, but that need not render the New Testament impressions of Transformation/Salvation in Jesus wholly opaque for today.

One such area, or I should say interconnected set of areas, where the recovery of the humanity of Jesus is becoming highly resonant, is in the fields of anti-racism, antisemitism, and postcolonial theology. Once we have noticed the entanglement of Christian reflection about Jesus with (i) ancient patterns of imperialism within the Roman Empire and since; (ii) racism and colonialism; (iii) the unexamined dismissal of other religions, allied to Christian missionary expansion through the ages; (iv) cultural assumptions of patriarchy; and (v) the denigration of Judaism as the shadow side of Christianity's eventual turn towards becoming a wholly Gentile religion, then the time is ripe for major revisions in how we imagine the relevance of Jesus and his message of the Kingdom of God today. Other essays in this book open the door on these issues, and point out ways in which Christological thinking requires major revision. For example, if it is the case that "Every aspect of [the British] Empire was an aspect of Christ", as has been documented in James Morris's three-volume history of the British Empire, then it is clear that a revision of Christian thought concerning the theological labels and metaphysical estimates traditionally surrounding the person Jesus of Nazareth is sorely needed.[26] Black Theology, Postcolonial Theology, Feminist Theology, Interreligious Theology, all embrace a higher regard for the humanity of the Jesus figure than has been the case in Christology's past life, and place a premium on dismantling what could be termed Christianity's "superiority complex" embedded in much traditional Christology. Furthermore, such dismantling will need to face the disingenuousness of some versions of Christian mission covered by the liberal-sounding term "inculturation", as has been sharply pointed out by the Aboriginal writer, Glenn Loughrey: "Jesus entered our world through the invasion and the action of those who ran the missions to which we were sent . . . All attempts to indigenize Jesus are simply neocolonialism, colonialism in different clothes."[27]

There are advantages in approaching the person and place of Jesus in Christian faith by exploring how it is that figures of history achieve heightened significance. In particular, it rescues us from the philosophical problem-solving mentality that has dogged discussion about the Christological two natures of Jesus for centuries. It keeps us close to the critical historical exploration of the impact of Jesus through New Testament studies, and it allows the fruits of those explorations to be felt in other areas of Christian theology and life, such as the ever-expanding area marked Christology.

---

[26] James Morris, *Heaven's Command: An Imperial Progress* (London: Faber and Faber, 1968), p. 319. John Hick comments on Morris's reading of imperial history as follows: "it is, I think, clear that in the eighteenth and nineteenth centuries the conviction of the decisive superiority of Christianity infused the imperial expansion of the West with a powerful moral impetus and an effective religious validation without which the enterprise might well have not been psychologically viable." See "The Non-Absoluteness of Christianity", in John Hick and Paul Knitter (eds), *The Myth of Christian Uniqueness: Toward a Pluralistic Theology of Religions* (Maryknoll, NY: Orbis Books and London: SCM Press, 1987), p. 20.

[27] Glenn Loughrey, "Jesus Through Indigenous Australian Eyes", in Gregory C. Jenks (ed.), *Cultural Afterlives of Jesus: Jesus in Global Perspective 3* (Eugene, OR: Wipf & Stock, 2023), pp. 7–21, here at p. 9.

4

Who do you say that I am?
Christology in feminist perspective
(or why feminist theologians should
continue to speak about Jesus)

Natalie K. Watson

Christology is central to Christian theology, yet many feminist theologians gradually lost interest in the debate about the person and nature of Jesus Christ. I discuss some feminist approaches to Jesus and Christology, and argue for the ongoing need to engage in this debate, to define the hermeneutical horizons of a contemporary Christological debate, and to realize its liberating potential for women.

For Christian theology to be true to its mission and to be the liberating force it can and needs to be, we cannot give up theology's most central task, to speak of Jesus Christ. Yet for many feminist theologians, the fact that a male human being is at the centre of the Christian faith became the kind of stumbling block of which both Jesus and Paul speak in different ways. For many, the scandal was not only that women were by and large excluded from the major Christological debates of the early Christian centuries, but more importantly that the maleness of Christ had become a force for the oppression and exclusion of women in the Church. Yet, I argue that speaking of Christ is too important a task in the endeavour of Christian theology to give up on and that it has in it the liberating power which feminist theologians seek to advocate.

Yet there is no doubt about it—Christianity is inherently scandalous: it has at the heart of its belief and practice something that can be hard to swallow. This is of course not a recent discovery, but it was none other than the apostle Paul who pointed this out to the congregation at the seaport of Corinth,[1] back then a veritable supermarket of religions, beliefs, practices, sects, and claims to know, or even to own, the truth. To some members of the earliest Christian communities, the idea that God would become a human being and would die what was regarded a most humiliating death on a cross was indeed a stumbling block.

And from these beginnings one could view the history of Christian theology as an attempt not only to articulate, define, and express what Christians actually believed about God, but also as a history of attempting to make palatable, to domesticate this scandal and confine in concepts and in words what is at the end of the day utterly beyond words: the Word that became flesh and dwelt among us, God who did "not abhor the virgin's womb", "to deliver man", God who was born, lived and died as a human being "for us . . . men . . . and for our salvation".

Maybe these snippets of traditional language still used by many in Christian worship indicate something else: that closely connected to this attempt to domesticate, to control, the *skandalon* of the incarnation and the cross, or even what Christians believe and teach about the Son of God, is another, that of not only our image of God, but our understanding of what it means to be human and how we understand the humanity God took upon himself. And perhaps also what this might mean for the place and the relationships of particular human beings within the Church, which was after all called "the body of Christ" by the apostle Paul.[2]

---

[1]   1 Corinthians 1:23.

[2]   1 Corinthians 12:12.

Male saviour—An insurmountable obstacle?

In the last three decades of the twentieth century, following the emergence of secular movements for the liberation of women on the one hand, and developments within the Church such as the Second Vatican Council, the rise of so-called theologies of liberation in Latin America and other parts of the world, and the ordination of women in some Protestant denominations, on the other hand, feminist theology emerged as an attempt to interrogate and rearticulate the core beliefs and practices of Christianity in the light of the experience of women. This is of course a shorthand for a multifaceted movement of many different voices and contexts: theological and philosophical approaches that had at their heart not to speak with one voice, but to make a greater diversity of voices heard and, perhaps most fundamentally, to challenge who decided what mattered enough to be called Christian theology and who was allowed to speak about it.

For some feminist writers on matters theological, the male saviour at the heart of Christian theology was an insurmountable obstacle, the stumbling block, the *skandalon*, the apostle Paul talked about, though perhaps for different reasons than those envisaged or encountered by Paul himself. For the early feminist theologians, this was the very embodiment of patriarchy itself, and therefore central to the need for women to recognize that Christianity was irredeemably patriarchal, with the consequence that the only possible response for women was to reject it. "If God is male," Mary Daly wrote, "then the male is God."[3] She accused Christians of Christolatry, and argued that women did not actually need a saviour, certainly not a male one. The Christianity the British theologian Daphne Hampson rejects is essentially Christologically focused: at the heart of Christianity is God's revelation as a male human being, and this male human being is given a status which no woman can attain. As Hampson wrote: "Christianity is a historical religion, one which

---

[3]   Mary Daly, *Beyond God the Father: Towards a Philosophy of Women's Liberation* (Boston, MA: Beacon Press, 1973), p. 19.

necessarily relates to history. And the history to which it relates is a patriarchal history."[4]

One of the most significant stories in the Gospels is Jesus's question to his disciples: "Who do you say that I am?"[5] The answer matters, and the "right" answer is a response not of knowledge but of faith, and the search for an answer to this question would remain central, if not the most central task, to Christian theology. This is not the place to repeat the history of the early Christian controversies in search of understanding and articulating how we speak about Jesus as both divine and human, God and "man", and what we do when we worship him as such. Yet, what is important is to point out that the history of searching for an answer to Jesus's question, "Who do you say that I am?", does not end with Peter's answer, and neither does it end with the Council of Chalcedon in 451 CE and its decision that Jesus is fully human and fully divine. Feminist theologians have identified the history of seeking an answer to this question as one of male privilege—even before we begin to discuss the significance of the maleness of Jesus Christ, being male is deemed essential to participation in the construction of orthodoxy, and little to no room is given to listen to the voices and the experience of women. In her article on Christology in the 1996 *Dictionary of Feminist Theologies*, Francine Cardman describes feminist Christology as "Decentring the Classical Tradition", "Contextualizing Women's Experience of Jesus" and "Relocating Christology: Christic Community".[6] If we identify the history of classical Christology as one of male privilege in which a male (clerical) elite defines how the discourse is shaped and women's experience and participation is at best deemed heretical and at worst rendered insignificant, then new and different questions would need to be asked: did the saviour need to be male? And how do women engage with the fact that he probably was?

---

4   Daphne Hampson, *Theology and Feminism* (Oxford: Blackwell, 1990), p. 9.

5   Mark 8:27–30; Matthew 16:13–20; Luke 9:18–22.

6   Francine Cardman, "Christology", in Letty M. Russell and J. Shannon Clarkson (eds), *Dictionary of Feminist Theologies* (Louisville, KY: Westminster John Knox Press, 1996), pp. 40–3.

In our feminist theological engagement with Christological discourses ancient and modern, we need also to engage critically with the anthropology behind any form of Christology: if Jesus Christ was human and maleness was an essential part of his humanity, how is humanity understood and what kind of patterns of gender construction does it entail?

One could begin with reworking the theological anthropology that is behind high patriarchal Christology, essentially the work of gender deconstruction, which values and affirms difference and regards the incarnation as a challenge to culturally defined oppressive gender constructions that regard women as inferior, as other: "A multi-polar anthropology allows Christology to integrate the maleness of Christ using interdependence of difference as a primary category, rather than emphasizing sexuality in an ideological, distorted way."[7]

However, for those of us who want to stay engaged in Christian theology and indeed in the life and practice of the Church, Christianity's seemingly inevitable compromise with patriarchy must not in itself become the ultimate stumbling block, nor should its persistent exclusion of women from formal theological discourse about who Christ is—whether he is human or divine, both fully human and fully divine—be accepted as a *fait accompli* or even a foregone conclusion. So, alongside outright rejection, we need to consider two further approaches by feminist theologians to respond to this problem of Christology: reclaiming and reimagining.

Reclaiming and reimagining

Reclaiming begins with the premise that for Christian feminist theologians the Christian tradition is too important to reject it outright, but what we need to do is to take our rightful place in the task of reading and rereading its sources and to make many different voices heard in its articulation and the practice and embodiment of its saving truth.

---

[7]   Elizabeth A. Johnson, "The Maleness of Christ", in Elizabeth Schüssler Fiorenza (ed.), *The Power of Naming: A Concilium Reader in Feminist Liberation Theology* (London: SCM Press, 1996), p. 311.

Reclaiming can take many different forms. For some, it began with a rereading of the earliest sources about Jesus and finding in them a Jesus who was a "protofeminist", someone who gathered around himself a movement of men and women who, contrary to the general tendency at their time, proclaimed the radical equality of men and women and as a consequence equal participation of men and women in all aspects of its practice. This is in many ways based on an anachronistic reading of history and does not really resolve any of the issues at hand. Does it really matter if Jesus, based on what we know from the sources in hand, was a "feminist"? An apocryphal story has it that one theologian responded to Leonard Swidler, one of the protagonists of this approach: "Even if Jesus was not a feminist, I am."[8]

The Roman Catholic feminist theologian Rosemary Radford Ruether perhaps rather poignantly formulated the question: "Can a male saviour save women?" Here she highlights one of the issues at stake: if Jesus is fully human, does this mean that his humanity is also subject to the restrictions of sex and gender, that God incarnate had to be male and that his maleness is part of what saves both men and women? For Ruether at the time, "what saves" is that Jesus becomes a human being who prefigures what redeemed humanity will be in an eschatological world of radical equality.[9]

For others, the focus shifts away from Jesus the male saviour to his mother Mary as the woman close to God, a woman who is truly our sister. Mary could be identified as a woman who had become rendered an idol of patriarchy, a demure submissive female who obeys the divine male without question and even her son, who embodies all culturally conditioned ideals of the submissive feminine and yet is what no woman can ever be, both virgin and mother, thus making her immaculately conceived body a substitute idol for the need to encounter real women's bodies. Instead, feminist theologians came to encounter Mary as a woman who had experienced what many of them were experiencing:

---

[8]   Cf. Leonard Swidler, *Jesus Was a Feminist: What the Gospels Reveal About His Revolutionary Perspective* (Lanham, MD: Sheed & Ward, 2007).

[9]   Rosemary Radford Ruether, *Sexism and God Talk: Towards a Feminist Theology* (Boston, MA: Beacon Press, 1983).

a single mother in a patriarchal society, and yet a leader in some of the earliest Christian communities, a forerunner for their own struggle for liberation.[10]

And yet, the question remains: what does it mean that at the heart of Christian theology is a male saviour? What does it mean for women, and how has the way this doctrine has been articulated throughout Christian history shaped the experience of women and men? Who is Christ and whose Christ is it?

Here we could begin with the experience of exclusion and rejection: if Christ is male, then only a man can rightly represent him at the altar, an argument still used to exclude women from the priesthood in main/malestream Christian denominations such as the Roman Catholic Church and perhaps complemented by somewhat dubious ideas of male headship in some Protestant denominations.

Elisabeth Schüssler Fiorenza's major contribution to the feminist theology of the 1980s was her pioneering *In Memory of Her: A Feminist Reconstruction of Christian Origins*.[11] In it, she identifies the earliest Christian communities as a movement of women and men gathered to remember and continue the radical memory of Jesus as God's wisdom living among us. These communities of Jesus-Sophia are the archetype for the *ekklesia* of women, the Church in which women speak of Christ and embody his memory. It is a hermeneutical space which women claim for themselves, and it challenges Christianity's compromise with patriarchy/kyriarchy in which male God-language and imagery becomes

---

[10] Cf. Elizabeth A. Johnson, *Truly Our Sister: A Theology of Mary in the Communion of Saints* (London: Continuum, 2003); and also e.g. Rosemary Radford Ruether, *Mary: The Feminine Face of the Church* (London: SCM Press, 1979); Ann Loades, *Searching for Lost Coins* (London: SPCK, 1987); María Clara Bingemer and Ivone Gebara, *Mary: Mother of God, Mother of the Poor* (London: Burns & Oates, 1989); Els Maeckelberghe, *Desperately Seeking Mary: The Feminist Reappropriation of a Religious Symbol* (Kampen: Pharos, 1991); Ann Loades, *Grace is Not Faceless: Reflections on Mary*, ed. and intro. by Stephen Burns (London: Darton, Longman & Todd, 2021).

[11] Elisabeth Schüssler Fiorenza, *In Memory of Her: A Feminist Reconstruction of Christian Origins* (London: SCM Press, 1983).

prevalent and is used to marginalize women. To create this hermeneutical space becomes the task of feminist theology:

> Feminist theology must rearticulate the symbols, images, and names of Divine Sophia in the context of our own experiences and theological struggles in such a way that the ossified and absolutized masculine language about G*d and Christ is radically questioned and undermined and the Western cultural sex-gender system is radically deconstructed. A feminist exegetical attempt to reconstruct the traces of Sophia as emancipatory Christology invites us to develop a critical praxis of reflective sophialogy.[12]

While the sources of the Christological debate which shaped the history of early Christianity, such as the works of the Church Fathers and the councils of the Church, are exclusively written by men and reflect a debate which may have been about matters of life and death but in which women nonetheless had no part, women have at different times and in different ways reflected on Christ. An example might be Julian of Norwich, fourteenth- and fifteenth-century English anchoress. In her *Revelations of Divine Love*, she records her desire to understand the passion of Christ:

> ... I thought I had already had some experience of the passion of Christ, but by his grace I wanted some more. I wanted to be actually there with Mary Magdalene and the others who loved him, and with my own eyes to see and know more of the physical suffering of our Saviour, and the compassion of our Lady and of those who there and then were loving him truly and watching his pains. I would be one of them and suffer with him.[13]

---

[12]   Elisabeth Schüssler Fiorenza, *Jesus: Miriam's Child, Sophia's Prophet* (London: SCM Press, 1995), p. 162. "G*d" was Fiorenza's substitution for the usual descriptor "God".

[13]   Julian of Norwich, *Revelations of Divine Love*, tr. Clifton Wolters (London: Penguin, 1966), p. 63 (Chapter 2).

This is but one example of the spirituality of medieval women who reflected on intimacy with Christ, and the crucified in particular. As Elizabeth Johnson wrote: "Women have consistently read themselves into the Christological mystery despite the patriarchal barricades that stand in the way."[14]

Another way in which this rereading might happen is by reimaging Christ as female. An example of this is Edwina Sandys's statue of the Christa which was briefly exhibited in the Cathedral of St John the Divine in New York in 1984, but was taken down because of the outrage it caused. The image is that of Christ as a crucified woman. The artist intended to draw attention to the suffering of women and knew that the statue would speak to women in a way religion often did not.[15] This is widely referred to in much of the literature on feminist theology in the 1990s.

Had Sandys gone a step too far? Reimagining Christ to reflect aspects of our own humanity and the way the human Christ relates to this is hardly something new. Matthias Grünewald's *Isenheim Altar* is regarded as one of the greatest works of Western art of the Middle Ages. In the crucifixion panel, the suffering of the crucified is vividly and graphically portrayed in his body being covered in scars that resemble those caused by a disease called St Anthony's Fever, an affliction suffered by the residents of the hospital for which the painting was originally created. Christ's body can be imagined as disfigured, despised, and rejected, as long as his maleness is left intact and visible. Pilgrims on the Camino de Santiago can visit the Chapel of the Most Holy Christ of Burgos which has at its centre a statue of the wounded Christ made in the fourteenth century and of Flemish origin. Devotion to this image spread far and wide throughout Spain and also to Latin America, where it is known as "Our Lord of Burgos". Here Christ is wearing what is very obviously a

---

[14]   Elizabeth A. Johnson, "Redeeming the Name of Christ", in Catherine Mowry LaCugna (ed.), *Freeing Theology: The Essentials of Theology in Feminist Perspective* (San Francisco, CA: Harper, 1993), p. 116.

[15]   <https://www.huffingtonpost.co.uk/entry/christa-edwina-sandys-art_n_57f55296e4b0b7aafe0b8999>, accessed 25 August 2023. See also Emma Schneider, "The Woman's Form", <https://medium.com/@emmasch/the-womans-form-ab1ea6ea9eef>, accessed 26 August 2023.

skirt, yet it is still a male Christ, thus the body of Christ is not disturbed by a woman's body. Another example of a reimagining of Christ as a suffering female is Margaret Argyle's *Bosnian Christa*, an image of a crucified woman inside a vulva, created in response to the suffering of countless women who were raped during the war in Bosnia-Herzegovina in the 1990s.[16]

Much has happened since the 1980s and 1990s when most of what could be called "feminist Christology" was written. Since then, two significant shifts have occurred. Feminist theologians increasingly took the "decentering" of theological discourse further and moved away from engagement with most of the classic theological subjects, to replace it with "eco-feminism". In the early 2000s, interest in feminism itself seemed to wane and was gradually replaced with a much wider debate around gender and identity that has had its impact on theology. So, is there still a place for feminist Christology in theological discourse today? And what would it need to look like?

Idoloclasm

Responding to Jesus's question "Who do you say that I am?" implies another question: "Who do you say you are?" From a feminist theological point of view, this means deconstructing and reconstructing what shapes our response to Christ's question, including the theologies which have instrumentalized the maleness of Christ, patriarchy/kyriarchy which has rendered women "other" and not fully human, and ontologically derived assertions whereby women are incapable of bearing God or representing Christ.

Perhaps the issue is not so much one of feminist theologians losing interest in Christology but rather a case for the deconstruction of "Christology as a doctrine which in its actual development has been used

---

[16]   See Julie Clague, "Interview with Margaret Argyle", *Feminist Theology* 10 (1995), pp. 57–68; the image can be seen online at <https://efecwomen. com/2017/12/13/date-announced-lecture-in-partnership-with-luther-king-house-12-february-2018/>, accessed 26 August 2023.

to reinforce women's subordination in the Church and hence in society".[17] This does not mean that feminist theologians should no longer speak about Jesus, as Jesus is too important not only for Christian theology but more importantly for the faith discourses of many women around the world. The task is therefore one of identifying how and in whose interest Christological doctrines have been and are being constructed, which traditions have been suppressed (such as the tradition of understanding Jesus as divine wisdom, so important in the reconstruction of an alternative reading of Christian origins), and to explore the impact of the symbolic language used on the actual lives of women. This is part of the task of idoloclasm, "feminist criticism's liberative 'breaking' of toxic imaginary figurations of the feminine".[18] This includes the deconstruction of toxic imaginations of the masculine, of identifying where the maleness of Christ has been used to project an image of a male God that is then instrumentalized to exclude and oppress women. As Melissa Raphael writes in her quest to reclaim the creative prophetic energy of Jewish and Christian feminist theologians: "By acts of idoloclasm, all women would be radically free: self-creative, self-legislating and, in that sense, divine."[19]

As the context changes and develops, so do the questions; therefore I would propose to identify some of the contexts in which the question about who Jesus is needs to be reframed today. What we can and need to do is to define and discover the hermeneutical spaces in which we can speak of Jesus Christ today.

"Who is Jesus Christ for us today?", asked Dietrich Bonhoeffer in 1944. "For us today" being the operative phrase here, we have already noted several shifts in understanding who Jesus is and the impact the context has had on these shifts in meaning. Yet, it is "for us" in a different sense, in the sense of "on our behalf", that is central to understanding the person and the work of Jesus. In their book *Saving Paradise: How*

---

[17]   Rosemary Radford Ruether, "Christology", in Lisa Isherwood and Dorothea McEwan (eds), *An A to Z of Feminist Theology* (Sheffield: Sheffield Academic Press, 1996), p. 26.

[18]   Melissa Raphael, *Religion, Feminism, and Idoloclasm: Being and Becoming in the Women's Liberation Movement* (London: Routledge, 2019), p. 11.

[19]   Raphael, *Religion, Feminism, and Idoloclasm*, p. 27.

Christianity Traded Love of This World for Crucifixion and Empire, Rita Nakashima Brock and Rebecca Ann Parker outline that in the Christian art of the first Christian millennium the crucifixion is rarely if ever depicted. The emphasis is not on the dying and dead Christ but on the living Christ who gives life to others. However, in the development of Christendom, Christianity's collusion with Empire, the understanding of the death of Christ as sacrificial becomes increasingly important, and "In Christianity's second millennium, Jesus as an abused and innocent victim, hanging dead on the cross, would become the image of holiness. But for a time—for nearly a thousand years—Christianity offered a different image of sanctity: the glory of God was humanity fully alive."[20] And thereafter individual penance and substitutionary atonement come to the fore, and women in particular are made aware of their need of penance. Julian of Norwich like other medieval mystics seeks to understand, to experience, the suffering of Christ on the cross, and she receives her "shewings" as her confessor holds a crucifix before her eyes, a scene that could well be understood as a form of spiritual abuse of a woman by a man in a position of religious power.

While in the Gospels, it is the women who are found under the cross, who stand with Christ in his suffering and who are the first to proclaim the good news of his resurrection, the collusion between Christianity, patriarchy, and empire—what Elisabeth Schüssler Fiorenza calls *kyriarchy*—has meant that women come to be understood as all that is sinful and in need of salvation and essentially redemption.

Christ With Us

The paradigm shift that a feminist reading of Christ can invoke is perhaps to move from asking what Christ did for us (men and for our salvation) to who and where Christ is with us. Suffering cannot be ignored; it is part of the reality of the lives of men, women, and children throughout

---

[20]   Rita Nakashima Brock and Rebecca Ann Parker, *Saving Paradise: How Christianity Traded Love of This World for Crucifixion and Empire* (Boston, MA: Beacon Press, 2008), p. 202.

history and throughout the world today. While some may have thought it presumptuous that a human being born of a woman could claim to be divine, the real *skandalon* of early Christianity was that God could become a human being, that God entered the reality of human life and thereby the reality of human suffering, and that includes the suffering of women.

The task of a feminist Christology is to find ways of speaking about the divinity and the full humanity of Christ in a way that acknowledges and affirms the full humanity of women. This theological discourse begins with the radical deconstruction of the abuse of the image of Christ that has denied the full humanity of women, that is, women as not being depicted in the image of God but essentially portrayed as a derivative of the male. While iconoclasts essentially seek to prevent the use of the icon as an object of worship in itself, as taking the place of that greater reality of which it seeks to be a mirror, idoloclasm deconstructs the abusive structures that render women other and make particular social constructions of gender, themselves sacrosanct and therefore a ready means for abuse.

What a feminist Christology can and must do is to identify and map out the theological horizon in which we speak of Christ who suffers with us, God who stands with us in our suffering and that of the whole of creation.

In a variety of different churches, neo-conservative "anti-gender" movements are on the rise, arguing for male headship or female submission, or insisting that only an able-bodied male can represent Christ at the altar. Those who insist that only a male priest can represent Christ make the validity of the sacrament dependent on one aspect of humanity, namely male sex, and therefore deny that the whole of humanity is created in the image of God and capable of representing God. This is in itself a form of idolatry. Thus there is an ongoing need for idoloclasm. Perhaps Mary Daly, who herself wrote about a need for the "breaking of idols", had a point.

How can we speak of a male Christ in the light of increasing awareness of sexual and spiritual abuse in the Church? The naming of sexual abuse as prevalent throughout Christian churches has thrown the Church, particularly in developed Western countries, into a fundamental crisis of credibility that goes deeper than the challenge of secularization. The betrayal of victims and survivors as well as the widespread collusion, be it out of ignorance or in the interest of institutional self-protection, is a deep wound, a trauma for the whole body of Christ. As during the AIDS crisis in the 1980s some advocated that "the body of Christ has AIDS", we must now say that the body of Christ has suffered and continues to suffer abuse. Therefore we need to search for a trauma-informed theology in which those who belong to the body of Christ, the Church, can learn to speak of their faith in a way that enables them to name their experience. This includes the way we speak of Jesus Christ, and a feminist trauma-informed theology for our time needs to find ways of naming Christ as the one who has himself suffered abuse and in whose name this abuse has been committed. The earliest Christian communities articulated their theology out of the experience of trauma and loss of and searching for identity, and including the destruction of the temple as well as the suffering, death, and resurrection of Jesus.

How can we speak of Christ in the shadow of the impending ecological disaster? Earlier in this chapter, I mentioned that by and large feminist theologians lost interest in matters of Christology and turned their attention to ecotheology. While I would want to make the case for speaking about Christ as an ongoing call to all engaged in Christian theology, we cannot ignore the fact that the eco-catastrophe is part of the reality of the world we live in, and its impact on women and children throughout the world is particularly severe. Therefore it needs to be part of the hermeneutical space we inhabit. Asian feminist theologians like Chung Hyun Kyung have spoken about the importance of suffering for their doing of feminist theology. Jesus as the suffering servant suffers alongside women and children affected by war, migration, and climate change.

What does it mean to engage in a transgressive Christology in an interfaith and multifaith world? The early feminist theologians of the 1970s and 1980s were frequently accused of anti-Judaism, not least in the context of male-dominated German academic theology, and scholars like Elisabeth Schüssler Fiorenza and Katharina von Kellenbach responded to this challenge. Much of this debate took place in the context of doctrine and the search for orthodoxy, yet feminist theology has deep roots in liberation theology which speaks of the primacy of praxis and practice, and thus it needs to engage and re-engage with women's discourses of faith which are often not confined by one male-defined religion but combine multiple practices of faith, orthopraxy, and transgressive practice. The Asian American theologian Rita Nakashima Brock for example writes about the importance of her Buddhist roots for developing her theology.[21] Recent scholarship about early Christianity emphasizes that parallel practices of Judaism and Christianity may well have existed into the second and third centuries. "Who do you say that I am?" What would a feminist Christopraxis in a multifaith world look like?

The task of Feminist Christology

The question that arises is this: if there is still a need for a feminist Christology, even several decades after the waning of feminist theological scholarship, what would its task be? We could conclude that the feminist scholars of the 1980s and 1990s have written Christology itself out of theological mainstream discourse and later scholars have focused on other subjects, such as ecotheology. Yet for Christian theologians, the question remains: "Who do you say that I am?" Elisabeth Schüssler Fiorenza in her work on Jesus-Sophia highlighted the importance of naming the hermeneutical space in which theological discourse happens and insisted on women claiming and reclaiming the power of naming. For the liberation theologians of the last decades of the twentieth century, Jesus was the liberator, the one who led the struggle of liberation for the poor and empowered them to join and shape this struggle for themselves. Therefore the challenge that remains for women theologians is to enter the space of the Gospel encounter between Jesus's question to his disciples, Peter's reply, and Jesus's commission to Peter, "You are Peter, and on this rock I will build my church".[22] As a feminist theologian of the twenty-first century, I want to ask what the purpose of articulating a Christology would be. The imperial intervention in the Christological

---

[21]   Rita Nakashima Brock and Rebecca Ann Parker, *Saving Paradise.*

[22]   Matthew 16:15–20.

controversies of the fourth century led not only to the articulation and settlement of what would be understood as orthodox theology but also to the consolidation of imperial power with the help of Christianity and thus essentially to the consolidation of patriarchal power within the Church and the empire. Thus we would need to ask what purpose our naming of Jesus Christ at the heart of the Christian faith and the Church would serve and who is granted the power of naming. In the early 1990s, Elisabeth Schüssler Fiorenza wrote:

> I argue that within the logic and rhetoric of radical democracy we can conceptualize the ekklēsia of wo/men as the metaphoric space that can sustain critical practices of struggle for transforming societal religious kyriarchal institutional discourses.[23]

The task of feminist speaking of God remains, and in the context of Christian theology this means speaking of God incarnate in a way that enables women, and all of humanity, to flourish and to conceive of their own lives as being in the image of God. This can mean an attempt to reappropriate and reconstruct Christological language, in order to speak of Christ as the liberator and of God who becomes a human being, thereby challenging by his very being established patriarchal gender constructions. In this way, women become liberators themselves, as they free themselves to be the human beings God created them to be, and in the process they overcome their "othering" as object and inferior, and finally represent in themselves the God who created them and who nourishes the whole of humanity. This is an ongoing endeavour; the work of a feminist theologian is never done. It means to create and work at communities of faith that are spaces of liberation for women and all human beings, communities of divine wisdom incarnate which continue to make counter-cultural claims on the world in which we live, and communities which continue the work of the "God-bearer" by bearing God ourselves in our bodies.

In my own work on feminist ecclesiology, I concluded that ultimately there could not be one model of Church which would suit the needs

---

[23] Fiorenza, *Jesus: Miriam's Child, Sophia's Prophet*, p. 28.

of feminist theologians better than another, thus critiquing the use of liberation theology and its concept of base ecclesial communities as models for feminist communities of liberation.[24] I argued that there was nothing inherently feminist in liberation theology as such, and that what liberation theology in its classical form hadn't done was to address the needs and concerns of women and children. Instead I proposed a framework of criteria which could be used to analyze and evaluate all forms of ecclesiology past, present and future from a feminist theological point of view. This could be a way forward for a continued feminist engagement with Christology. Melissa Raphael revisits the idoloclasm of second wave feminism "as a means of revisiting the prophetic energy of feminism".[25]

Feminist theology is essentially theology that seeks to create communities of justice. Does our speaking of Christ enable such justice to happen? Do we see the story of the triune God embodied in the stories of women's lives, and can we speak of God incarnate in a way that enables women to speak their stories and to hear each other into speech? Is our Christology one of a Church that is an embodied community which enables the proclamation of God in Word and Sacrament in the lives of women? Is the way we speak of the particularity of Jesus's human life open to celebrating the richness of difference and diversity in our lives and in the life of the Church as a whole?

"Who do you say that I am?" Who do you think you are? Speaking of Christ at the beginning of the third Christian millennium still begins with claiming a place at the table, claiming that women throughout history and throughout the world have borne God and named Christ, and that

---

[24]   See Natalie K. Watson, *Introducing Feminist Ecclesiology* (London: Continuum, 2002); "Feminist ecclesiology", in Gerard Mannion and Lewis S. Mudge (eds), *The Routledge Companion to the Christian Church* (New York and London: Routledge, 2008), pp. 461–75. See also, "The Place Where Love is Possible: A Feminist Relational Attempt to Rethink the Cross", in Lisa Isherwood and Elaine Bellchambers (eds), *Through Us, With Us, In Us: Relational Theologies in the Twenty-First Century* (London: SCM Press, 2010), pp. 212–29.

[25]   Raphael, *Religion, Feminism and Idoloclasm*, p. 34.

this is indeed theology, part of the Church's body of language seeking to speak the ineffable, to name the mystery of the Word made flesh.

It means to recognize that what we speak about ultimately cannot be contained in human language and imagination, but human language and imagination is what we have at our disposal, and therefore we have to use it wisely and for good, for our good, the good of the whole Church, and of the whole world.

Icons are images that are windows to the divine reality: they are not objects of worship themselves, but enable the worshipper to see beyond and to be seen. Feminist theology has to recognize its limitations, to know that ultimately our speaking of God will be limited by our own political and hermeneutical horizons. What we can speak about is within those political and hermeneutical horizons, and the way we do so will be shaped by the way we imagine God to be. What we can speak about is ourselves and the world around us, creation, human and non-human. How we speak about Christ, the God who has become human so that human beings may become divine, reflects on how we think about our own humanity and that of others. Moving beyond the question of whether women can represent Christ at the altar, we can therefore ask if our Christology is such that we can imagine women as icons of Christ, whether women's humanness is indeed capable of being a window on the divine. Do we imagine ourselves and all human beings as being born into the fullness of the humanity God embraced, or do we allow one aspect of that humanity to dominate, to obscure our vision of the divine, to become a tool for exclusion and oppression rather than liberation, whether we can indeed see the glory of God in a woman fully alive?

5

Jesus Christ under Hindu gaze

Anantanand Rambachan

Although the Christian tradition has had a long presence in India and interacted with Hindu traditions, this engagement intensified with the arrival of the colonial powers and the missionaries who accompanied them. Dialogue deepened and Hindus were challenged to respond to Christianity. Most of the Hindu leaders and commentators, with rare exceptions, embraced Jesus on Hindu terms, but turned away from the institution of the Church and its doctrines and especially from the exclusive claims made for Jesus. In affirming the significance of Jesus, each Hindu thinker gave importance to a different facet of Jesus's life and teaching. All commended Jesus's theocentric life and the centrality of his ethics. Others highlighted his renunciation and otherworldliness. There is a consensus that Hindus had much to learn from Jesus's life and teachings.

Although there are traditions that connect the apostle St Thomas with India, and evidence of a Christian presence in South India from the seventh or eighth centuries CE, we have no records of Hindu–Christian interaction prior to the colonial period. The European quest for products and trade routes in the seventeenth century brought merchants from Portugal and Britain to India, and Christian missionaries were not slow in following. The British East India Company, which exercised control of significant portions of Indian territory from the 1750s, was initially reluctant to allow missionaries to proselytize in India. Company officials were concerned that the work of missionaries would stir hostility among Hindus and impede business prospects. The Company's charter, however, was revised in 1813 and again in 1833, removing obstacles to missionary work in its territories.

From its earliest days, the Christian tradition in India was diverse and distinguished by national origin, theology, liturgy, and culture. The oldest community, the Thomas Christians, traced by some Indian Christian traditions to the arrival of the apostle Thomas in the first century, was concentrated in the region of Kerala and maintained generally cordial relations with Hindu neighbours. Roman Catholic communities (c. fifteenth century CE) were concentrated in the Portuguese enclaves, but present in smaller numbers elsewhere. Beginning in the eighteenth century, Protestant missionaries commenced work in India and by the nineteenth century the largest and most influential Christian communities comprised European and American Protestant denominations. These groups had the more significant dialogical encounters with the Hindu tradition.

It was in the region of Bengal, in the eighteenth and nineteenth centuries, where the Christian tradition made its greatest impact in India, coinciding with the establishment of British control in the same area. There were many influential missionaries whose work had reverberations in the Hindu community and contributed to the development of Hindu–Christian interactions. One of these was William Carey (1761–1834). Carey, a pioneer in the foundation of the Baptist Missionary Society, operated first from a Danish enclave near Calcutta. He enlisted the help of traditional Hindu scholars to assist him with the work of translating the Bible into Indian languages. The publication of a Bengali version of the New Testament in 1801 was followed by the translation of large parts of the Bible into the languages of India. Carey's methods for the spread of Christianity in India included traditional preaching, education, and the above-mentioned translation and distribution of Christian literature in local languages.

Although missionaries successfully converted many educated Hindus to Christianity, it is likely that they did not anticipate perhaps the most important outcome of exposure to Christianity and Western education. Education had the effect also of turning Hindus back to their own tradition, seeking a clearer and deeper understanding of its insights. These Hindus were among the principal agents for the renewal and reinvigoration of the Hindu tradition. They engaged in vigorous debates with their Christian contemporaries and are among the earliest participants and shapers of Hindu–Christian dialogue. The lives of these pioneers of Hindu–Christian dialogue exemplify the profound way in which an encounter with another tradition can transform and enrich one's understanding of his or her home tradition.

Most of the Hindu leaders were inspired by and learned from Jesus. They drank deeply from his teachings and his embodiment of the meaning of an awakening to God for our lives in this world and our human relationships. At the same time, they had considerable difficulty with institutionalized Christianity. A significant part of the problem here is the alliance they experienced between the institution of the Church and colonial rule. Many, in fact, used the teachings and example of Jesus to chastise the Church and what they saw as the chasm between the ideals of Jesus and Christian practice. They commended and contrasted Jesus's freedom from greed, his non-possessiveness, and his generous self-giving with the affluence of the Church and the materialism of some Christians. Let us turn to a few prominent Hindu leaders and their engagement with Jesus and Christianity.

Raja Ram Mohan Roy

The earliest and one of the most influential Hindus in this regard was Ram Mohan Roy (1772–1833). Roy was born into an orthodox Brahmin Hindu family in the village of Radhanagar, Bengal. He studied Islam at Patna and Hinduism in Varanasi but became disenchanted with his ancestral tradition. Service in the East India Company and the Bengal Civil Service gave Roy exposure to the English language and to British politics, administration, culture, and religion. In 1829, Roy founded the Brahmo Sabha (subsequently called the Brahmo Samaj), for the reform and regeneration of Hindu society. Between the years 1829 and 1884, the Brahmo Samaj, though numerically small, was the centre of all progressive religious and social movements and exerted considerable influence. The movement produced a series of charismatic leaders who determined its doctrine and direction.

In 1820, Roy published *The Precepts of Jesus*, a collection of what Roy considered to be Jesus's ethical teachings. Roy clarified his intention in words that are often quoted:

> These precepts separated from the mysterious dogmas and historical records, appear, on the contrary, to the compiler to contain not only the essence of all that is necessary to instruct mankind in their civil duties, but also the best and only means of obtaining forgiveness of sins, the favor of God and strength to overcome our passions and to keep his commandments.[1]

Roy believed that the ethical teachings of Jesus offered resources for the reform of Hindu society and that these teachings could be distinguished from the doctrines of the Church about Jesus. What Roy included in his selection from the Gospel is as significant as what he chose to omit. He omitted biographical passages and references to the miracles of Jesus, in large part because the historical dimension does not have the same significance for liberation (*moksha*) in the Hindu tradition as it does for Christians. The differing valuation of the historical, here underlined by Roy through exclusion, is a continuing thread in the Hindu understanding of Jesus.

I am not sure what response Roy expected from his Christian missionary friends. Perhaps he anticipated support for his commendation of Jesus's teaching to Hindus, or an invitation to continuing dialogue. The response was one of condemnation and hostility. At the heart of the Christian response to Roy was the accusation that he focused on the ethical teachings of Jesus to the exclusion of the central claim of these texts that salvation is possible only through the atoning sacrifice of Jesus on the cross. Though holding Jesus in high esteem, "superior even to the angels in heaven", Roy did not share the traditional Christian understanding of Jesus as identical with God. He argued that Jesus himself had a theocentric understanding of his relationship with God. On this

---

[1]   Cited in M. M. Thomas, *The Acknowledged Christ of the Indian Renaissance* (Madras: Christian Literature Society, 1970), p. 10. Original, *English Works of Raja Rammohan Roy* (Allahabad, 1906), p. 552.

issue Roy differs from later Hindus who are more willing to consider the divinity of Jesus but reject the exclusivity of such claims. In rejecting the divinity of Jesus, Roy was consistent since he also denied the Hindu doctrine of divine descent (*avatar*).

Keshub Chunder Sen

Keshub Chunder Sen (1838–84) inherited the mantle of Brahmo Samaj leadership from Ram Mohan Roy. His distinctive contribution to Hindu discourse about Jesus is his introduction of the idea of the Asiatic Christ. This idea resonated later in the exposition of leading Hindu voices like Swami Vivekananda and Mahatma Gandhi, but the idea was first enunciated in an eloquent and wide-ranging lecture delivered on 5 May 1866, in Calcutta.[2] Sen began his lecture with a description of Jesus as "the greatest and truest benefactor of mankind". He painted a gloomy picture of human civilization prior to the birth of Jesus, describing the world as "deep in the gloom of ignorance and corruption". Jesus Christ was thus a necessity of the age: he appeared in the fullness of time. And, certainly, no great man ever rose in the world, but his birth was necessitated by surrounding circumstances, and his life was a necessary response to the demands of the age.

Sen traced the history of the Church from its periods of early persecution and martyrdom to the time of Constantine when Christianity became the religion of the empire. Political power, he argued, resulted in corruption, and created the conditions for the work of Luther. He sketched the history of Christianity in India, building his speech to a rhetorical question that was greeted with applause: "Is there a single soul in this large assembly who would scruple to ascribe extraordinary moral heroism to Jesus Christ and him crucified?"[3]

Sen spoke of the gratitude of India for Christianity and of British political control as the expression of divine will, while lamenting the

---

[2] S. D. Collett (ed.), *Lectures and Tracts by Keshub Chunder Sen* (London: Strahan, 1870).

[3] Collett, *Lectures and Tracts*.

rancour, hatred, and mutual stereotyping that characterized relationships between Indians and English people. After calling European attention to their oppression of natives, Sen spoke of their "muscular Christianity", which caused Indians to identify the tradition with power, privilege, and injustice: "Behold Christ crucified in the lives of those who profess to be his followers! Had it not been for them, the name of Jesus Christ would have been ten times more glorified than it seems to have been."[4]

It is at this point in his lecture that Sen introduced his idea of the Asiatic Christ, using it to affirm his dignity and self-worth as an Indian:

> I rejoice, yea, I am proud, that I am an Asiatic. And was not Jesus Christ an Asiatic? Yes and his disciples were Asiatics, and in Asia. When I reflect on this, my love for Jesus becomes a hundredfold intensified; I feel him nearer to my heart, and deeper in my national sympathies. Why should I then feel ashamed to acknowledge that nationality which he acknowledged? Shall I not rather say, he is more congenial and akin to my oriental nature, more agreeable to my Oriental habits of thought and feeling? And is it not true that an Asiatic can read the imageries and allegories of the Gospel, and its descriptions of natural sceneries, of customs and manners, with greater interest, and a fuller perception of their force and beauty, than Europeans?[5]

Like Roy before him, Sen claimed that his understanding of Jesus is independent of the Church, derived directly from his reading of the biblical texts. He also followed Roy in giving emphasis to the so-called ethical teachings of Jesus, especially those having to do with forgiveness and self-sacrifice.

---

4   Collett, *Lectures and Tracts.*
5   Collett, *Lectures and Tracts.*

Swami Dayananda Saraswati

Not all Hindu commentators, however, positively affirmed the significance of Jesus and his teachings. Swami Dayananda Saraswati (1824–83), founder of the reformist Arya Samaj organization, rejected entirely any claims to truth in Christianity and asserted the sole truth of his exposition of the teachings of the Vedas. He affirmed the Vedas to be the repository of eternal and universal truth. Dayananda introduced a quite different tone and content into the Hindu encounter with Christians and Christianity, contrasting sharply with figures like Roy and Sen. He understood the claims of Christianity as standing or falling on the authority of the Bible and developed his critique of the Christian tradition in his magnum opus, *Satyartha Prakash* (Light of Truth).[6]

The Bible, in Dayananda's view, ought not to be considered divine revelation, because its teachings are irrational, immoral, and untrue. Unlike the Vedas, the Bible does not propound eternal truths since its teachings are rooted in historical events. Dayananda was also critical of the image of God emerging from the biblical texts: bound by time and space, violent, jealous, and relying on miracles that are inconsistent with scientific truths. On the Christian doctrine of the Virgin Birth of Jesus, Dayananda is sarcastic, but includes similar Hindu narratives in his critique: "If the story of the birth of Christ were held to be true, any unmarried girl that happens to conceive could say that she was with child of the Holy Ghost. . . . This story is as possible as that recorded in the Puranas about Kunti being conceived of the Sun."[7]

In Dayananda, there is none of the esteem and respect for Jesus that we encountered earlier. He challenges the Christian understanding of Jesus as the Son of God, the truth of the miracles ascribed to Jesus, Jesus's resurrection from the grave, and atonement as a core Christian doctrine. Christians, according to Dayananda, were inconsistent in arguing for the miracles of Jesus while denying such claims in the Hindu tradition.

---

[6]   Dayananda Saraswati, *Light of Truth*, tr. C. Bharadwaja (Delhi: Arya Pratinidhi Sabha, 1975).

[7]   Saraswati, *Light of Truth*, p. 618.

Jesus, in Dayananda's view, is not a person who offers valuable religious teachings to Hindus and cannot serve as an exemplar of ethics.

Swami Vivekananda

Swami Vivekananda (1863–1902) is arguably the most influential interpreter of the Hindu tradition in recent times to both India and the West. In his eloquent speeches to the World Parliament of Religions (1893) and across the United States of America after the Parliament, Vivekananda both informed and defined: he shared what he regarded as the core teachings of the Hindu tradition and, in doing so, also gave the tradition a distinctive shape and definition. Although Vivekananda identified himself most closely with the worldview of the non-dual Advaita Vedanta tradition, he sought to comprehensively define the essential elements of the Hindu tradition and to offer an interpretation of the relationship obtaining among its different streams. His imprint on the understanding of the Hindu tradition by Hindus and others remains indelible.

After Hinduism, the tradition that engaged Swami Vivekananda's attention and thought most significantly was Christianity. There are many reasons for this. Swami Vivekananda inherited the history of the Brahmo Samaj's interest in Christ and Christianity. The Brahmo Samaj founder Ram Mohan Roy, and his successor Keshub Chandra Sen, spoke and wrote a great deal about Christianity. As a young man, Swami Vivekananda was active in the circles of the Brahmo Samaj. Vivekananda was educated at the Scottish Church College in Calcutta, an institution founded by the Christian missionary, Alexander Duff. One assumes that he would have had significant exposure to Christianity and even read Christian texts. Christian missionaries were active in Calcutta and often ignited controversies. Vivekananda developed a Christology based on his understanding of Advaita Vedanta, and it is important that we treat his views in more detail.

Vivekananda's earliest known views about Christ and Christianity were expressed in a preface that he wrote to his Bengali translation of *The Imitation of Christ*, a work attributed to the medieval Catholic

monk, Thomas à Kempis (*c*.1380–1471).[8] He translated six chapters
of this work, added appropriate quotations from Hindu texts and
contributed these to a Bengali monthly journal. *The Imitation of Christ*
engaged Vivekananda's attention in a special way, and it was the only
text, other than the Bhagavadgita, that he kept with him during his
years of travelling around India after the death of his revered teacher,
Sri Ramakrishna. Vivekananda translated and published *The Imitation
of Christ* in order to present Hindus with what he understood to be the
true spirit of Christianity. This spirit, Vivekananda felt, was absent from
the lives of most Christians whom Hindus encountered in day-to-day
situations. Missionaries, according to Vivekananda, spoke of the ideal of
renunciation, but this was never embodied in their lives. In commending
this text to Hindus, he argued that religious wisdom was not limited to
India but may be found among those regarded as inferior and impure.

The preface that Vivekananda wrote to his translation of *The Imitation
of Christ* is important because, besides being his earliest written work
(1889), four years before he spoke at the Parliament of Religions (1893),
it reflects faithfully the features of Christianity that he found attractive.
He could understand and identify with the author of this work whose
ideals and way of life closely resembled the aspirations and values of a
traditional Hindu renunciant. Vivekananda admired the author's radical
renunciation, his thirst for purity, and his unceasing spiritual effort.
Vivekananda likened *The Imitation of Christ* to the Bhagavadgita in its
spirit of complete self-surrender and saw the author as embodying the
Hindu ideal of devotion to God as a servant to a master. We see in this
preface what would be a central theme of Vivekananda's Christology:
Jesus as the model embodiment of renunciation.

Vivekananda presented his most detailed understanding of Jesus in a
lecture entitled "Christ, The Messenger", delivered in Los Angeles in 1900.
In this lecture, the core components of his Christology are identified, and
we will now consider the salient aspects.

---

[8]   See CW8: pp. 159–61. All references are taken from *The Complete Works of
        Swami Vivekananda* (abbreviated CW), 8 vols, Mayavati Memorial Edition
        (Calcutta: Advaita Ashrama, 1964–71). Volume and page numbers are
        indicated after the letters CW.

Jesus: The Otherworldly Renunciant

Vivekananda represents Jesus as entirely otherworldly, with no interest in this "evanescent world and its belongings".[9] He is critical of interpreters who have spoken of Jesus as a politician, a patriotic Jew or even a military leader. The Gospels, according to Vivekananda, offer no justification for such readings. He cites Matthew 8:20—"Foxes have holes, and birds of the air have nests, but the Son of Man has nowhere to lay his head"—as the best commentary on the life of Jesus. He speaks of Jesus as a "disembodied, unfettered, unbound spirit," with no consciousness of the physical body:

> He had no sex ideas! He was a soul! Nothing but a soul, just working a body for the good of humanity; and that was all his relation to the body. In the soul there is no sex. The disembodied soul has no relationship to the animal, no relationship to the body. The ideal may be far away beyond us. But never mind, keep to the ideal. Let us confess that it is our ideal, but we cannot approach it yet.[10]

Christ, according to Vivekananda, was a renunciant, and his teachings were meant to be followed only by renunciants. The world and life in the world, says Vivekananda, had no interest in Jesus. His only concern was to push it forward towards God and to enable everyone to realize their spiritual nature.

Vivekananda expressed great disappointment over the differences between the ideals of Jesus and the practices of some Christians in his time. He felt strongly that Christians had strayed far from the teachings of Jesus. In the city of Detroit on 21 February 1894, Vivekananda was fiery and eloquent and held before his audience the model of Jesus as a renunciant (*sannyasin*):

> You are not Christians. No, as a nation you are not. Go back to Christ. Go back to him who had nowhere to lay his head. "The

---

[9]   CW4, p. 144.

[10]   CW4, p. 145.

birds have their nests and the beasts their lairs, but the Son of Man has nowhere to lay his head." Yours is religion preached in the name of luxury. What an irony of fate! Reverse this if you want to live, reverse this. It is all hypocrisy that I have heard in this country. All this prosperity, all this from Christ! Christ would have denied all such heresies. If you can join these two, this wonderful prosperity with the ideal of Christ, it is well. But if you cannot, better go back to him and give this up. Better be ready to live in rags with Christ than to live in palaces without him.[11]

Jesus: The Ahistorical Teacher

Swami Vivekananda's characterization of Jesus as the teacher of a doctrine of otherworldliness is connected closely with another significant dimension of his Christology. This is his almost complete disinterest in the historical Jesus, a subject of central concern for the Christian tradition. In response to a question about the crucifixion of Jesus, his answer was direct and terse: "Christ was God incarnate; they could not crucify him. That which was crucified was only a semblance, a mirage."[12] Vivekananda seemed well aware of some of the scholarly disputes about the historical Jesus but attributes no significance to these. He spends little time wondering why this may be important to the Christian tradition. Historical truths appear to him to be non-essential. Vivekananda does not question Jesus's historicity but attributes no special significance to the connection between history and his religious significance:

> We are not here to discuss how much of the New Testament is true, we are not here to discuss how much of that life is historical. It does not matter at all whether the New Testament was written within five hundred years of his birth, nor does it matter even *how much of that life is true*. But there is something behind it, something we want to imitate.[13]

---

[11]   CW8, p. 213.

[12]   CW1, p. 328.

[13]   CW4, p. 146. My italics. It is of interest to note that Swami Vivekananda dismissed Nicholas Notovich's view that Jesus travelled to Tibet and was

Although Vivekananda is not interested in Christian claims for the historical Jesus, he is concerned to argue, like Keshub Chunder Sen, for the Asiatic nature of Christ. Vivekananda speaks of Jesus as a "true son of the Orient", possessing what he describes as a preference for the practical in matters religious. Echoing the words of Keshub Chunder Sen, Vivekananda speaks in almost identical terms about Jesus's identity:

> Many times you forget, also, that the Nazarene himself was still an Oriental. With all your attempts to paint him with blue eyes and yellow hair, the Nazarene was still an Oriental. All the similes, the imageries, in which the Bible is written—the scenes, the locations, the attitudes, the groups, the poetry and symbol— speak to you of the Orient: of the bright sky, of the heat, of the sun, of the desert, of the thirsty men and animals; of men and women coming with pitchers on their heads to fill them at the wells; of the flocks, of the ploughmen, of the cultivation that is going on around; of the water-mill and wheel, of the mill-pond, of the mill-stones. All these are to be seen today in Asia.[14]

The affirmation of Jesus's Asiatic identity was important to Swami Vivekananda because it enabled him to claim that Jesus is better understood in India than in the Western world. It was the ground also for challenging the Eurocentric focus of Christianity and arguing for the superiority of Asia in religious matters, in spite of Western political and military might.

Jesus: The Advaitin
Swami Vivekananda's otherworldly Jesus, whose significance will not be found in the facts of history, was pre-eminently a teacher of Advaita. Vivekananda's Christology was informed decisively by his theory of human religious evolution. For Vivekananda, the goal of this journey is the awakening to the non-dual reality underlying the universe and constituting the self (*atma*) of all. This awakening is available in all the

---

buried there after his death. See CW6, p. 359; CW3, p. 264.

[14]   CW4, p. 142.

religions of the world. Paths may be different, but the goal of non-duality is one and the same.

Vivekananda traces three stages in the development of all religions. In the first stage, God is understood as an extra-cosmic being, both omnipotent and omniscient. There is little human intimacy with God at this stage, and the emphasis is on divine transcendence. The second stage emphasizes panentheism. God is understood to be present not only in the heavens, but also in our world and, most importantly, in the human being. In the final stage of religious evolution, the human being discovers unity and identity with the all-pervasive, non-dual truth of the universe. All religions, according to Vivekananda, reflect these three phases since the evolution to a higher stage does not imply the discarding of any earlier phase.

Employing the Hindu teaching about the necessity of a teacher to relate his teaching to a student's religious aptitude, Vivekananda reads Jesus as teaching to three distinct types of disciples:

> To the masses who could not conceive anything higher than a Personal God, he said, "Pray to your Father in Heaven." To others who could grasp a higher idea, he said, "I am the vine you are the branches," but to his disciples to whom he revealed himself more fully, he proclaimed the highest truth, "I and my Father are One."[15]

Given Swami Vivekananda's overall view of human religiosity as culminating in non-duality and his understanding of Jesus as a teacher of this truth, it does not surprise that he gives particular importance to the Gospel of John and especially to those statements of Jesus that affirm unity with God and the realization of God within. The two texts most often cited by him are John 10:30, "The Father and I are one", and Luke 17:21, "The kingdom of God is among you". He interprets "The Father and I are one" "to have the same meaning as the Advaita great sentence, 'I am *brahman* (*aham brahmasmi*)."

---

[15]   CW2, p. 143.

Jesus: A State of Being

Jesus, for Vivekananda, like the Buddha, represents a state to be attained. In 1895, during an address at the Thousand Island Park in New York, Vivekananda spoke clearly on this:

> The Absolute cannot be worshipped, so we must worship a manifestation, such a one as has our nature. Jesus had our nature; he became the Christ; so can we, and so *must* we. Christ and Buddha were the names of a state to be attained; Jesus and Gautama were the persons to manifest it.[16]

Jesus became the Christ and Gautama the Buddha. It is the state that is important and not the historical person. The state is universal and eternal and not so the historical particularities of the person who attains it. One of the paramount errors of the Christian tradition in history, according to Swami Vivekananda, is that the messenger became the message. Christians lacked the insight to separate these two and the messenger, who cared not to be remembered or known, took centre stage. The aim of Christian life should not be to imitate Jesus, but to be Jesus. The potential to be as great as Jesus or Buddha is inherent in every human being. It does not surprise us that Swami Vivekananda exemplified minimal interest in the crucifixion and resurrection of Jesus or in Christian teaching about atonement. Atonement, or the claim that the death of Jesus opened the doorway to salvation, made no sense in the worldview of Vivekananda.

It is beyond the concern of this essay to offer an assessment of Vivekananda's Christology. What is clear is that Vivekananda does not set out to interpret the meaning of Jesus in the manner of a systematic Christian theologian or a biblical scholar. He has a clearly developed theoretical framework through which he reads the history of human religiosity and applies this to his understanding of Hindu and non-Hindu traditions. At the core of his approach is his view that religions reflect an evolutionary progression from dualism to panentheism that, in turn, culminates in non-dualism. Non-dualism (*advaita*) is the fulfilment and culmination of the human religious quest. From the panoramic vantage

---

[16] CW7, p. 29.

point of this Advaita theology of religions, Swami Vivekananda surveys the Christian tradition and interprets it in the light of his evolutionary theology. What Swami Vivekananda offers us is an Advaita view of Jesus that conforms to his understanding of religious evolution. As one commentator observed, "If Christians can speak of an unknown Christ of Hinduism, Hindus can speak of an unknown Vedanta of Christianity."[17]

A personal gaze

In my own case, it seems inevitable that I would know of Jesus from a very young age.[18] I grew up in an orthodox Hindu family in Trinidad, a small island of ethnic, cultural, and religious diversity in the southern Caribbean. Although my grandfathers were Hindu priests, it seems that they had no fear of or antagonism towards Christianity and did not perceive it as a threat to their identity. Their value for religion and the religious life extended to other traditions and their practitioners. Hindus are interested in the spiritual experiences of people of other faiths. We were permitted to participate in nativity plays in kindergarten and to join our friends at the local church for Sunday school. I will always remember how elated I felt when I answered what seemed to be an incredibly difficult question. We were asked to guess how long Joseph knocked on the innkeeper's door the night Jesus was born. Some of the unsuccessful answers attempted to quantify the number of knocks, while others gave specific length of time. Suddenly, I intuitively yelled "until the door was opened", and exulted in getting the answer that eluded my Christian friends!

Christian missionaries regularly called at our home to talk and to distribute literature. We politely listened, accepted, and occasionally read the material they left with us. At the Presbyterian high school where I received my secondary school education, there were further opportunities to hear of Jesus. I read the Gospels and made the effort to

---

[17]   Thomas, *The Acknowledged Christ*, p. 150.

[18]   For readers who are interested in a more detailed discussion of my views on Hindu–Christian relations see Anantanand Rambachan, *Pathways to Hindu–Christian Dialogue* (Minneapolis, MN: Fortress Press, 2022).

better understand Hinduism by reading works, in English, by modern commentators. I found the account of these writers full of admiration and warmth towards Jesus and the conviction of his importance. Sri Ramakrishna, the teacher of Swami Vivekananda, spoke of his mystical encounters with Jesus and the story of Jesus was read, by Vivekananda, for inspiration on the occasion of the inauguration of the Ramakrishna Mission, one of modern Hinduism's most important movements. Disciples of Swami Vivekananda recounted Vivekananda's impact:

> The meditation lasted long. When a break was made, Naren [childhood name for Vivekananda] began to tell the life story of the Lord Jesus, beginning with the wondrous mystery of his birth through his death and to his resurrection. Through the eloquence of Narendra, the boys were admitted into that apostolic world wherein Paul had preached the gospel of the Risen Christ and spread Christianity far and wide. Naren made his plea to them to become Christs themselves, and to aid in the redemption of the world; to realize God and to deny themselves as the Lord Jesus had done ... The very air seemed to vibrate with their ecstatic fervour. Strangely, the monks discovered afterwards that it was Christmas Eve.[19]

Hindu reflections sustained my interest in Jesus and helped me to look beyond the missionary zeal for proselytization and conversion and the representation of Jesus as condemning all religions.

Jesus's God-centreedness

What powerfully attracted me to Jesus, and I believe attracted Hindus from the time of Ram Mohan Roy, was his unmistakable awakening to and centredness in God. I found that the symbols and images, the examples and parables used by Jesus in talking about the religious life had a lot in common with Hindu texts and teachers. His words and actions were infused with an authenticity that spoke immediately to one's heart.

---

[19]   Eastern and Western Disciples, *The Life of Swami Vivekananda* (Calcutta: Advaita Ashrama, 1974), pp. 159–60.

Jesus lived in and for God. His rootedness in God manifested itself in a life lived without fear, and which, at depth, was full and peaceful. The fullness that Jesus experienced from his unity with God liberated him from greed and enabled him to live generously for others. This freedom was transparent in a lifestyle of non-possessiveness, his teaching about the limits of wealth and his condemnation of greed.

Compassion and justice

I was also drawn to the fact that the spirit of renunciation that infused the life of Jesus did not mean, as it too often does, a self-absorbed condition that exults in indifference and turning away from the world. One of my favourite parables of Jesus is the well-known one from Matthew 25:34–40 which equates righteousness with caring for those in need and overcoming estrangement. Jesus's teaching here is that knowledge and love of God is inseparable from the love of one's fellow human beings. One cannot be mindful of God and unmindful of the community of human beings in whom God exists. Love of God must find expression in a life of service and compassion. Jesus's passionate love and value for others, expressing his loving commitment to God, was the measure of differentiating authentic from inauthentic ways of being religious. An act of love on the Sabbath (Mark 2:27) is authentic and such actions are not limited to those who belong to our own communities. It may be expressed more fully in the story of the Good Samaritan (Luke 10:29–37) whose hero the parable assumes we are taught to despise and regard as impure. Love crosses traditional boundaries and enfolds those who are marginalized by gender, disease, hate, ethnicity, and cultural difference.

Jesus's understanding of God as infinite love, fullness and peace, and his conviction that God fulfils the deepest human longings, explain his extraordinary compassion. Although God is the end of all human seeking, we repeatedly turn to unsatisfactory substitutes, failing to find the meaning that we search for and hurting our fellow beings and ourselves. Jesus's final words from the cross, "Father, forgive them; for they do not know what they are doing" (Luke 23:32–4), never fails to move and draw me. It reveals a heart of compassion that has no space for violence and that finds no delight in vengeful crushing of the other. Human violence, on the other hand, has as its primary source a fundamental ignorance of the joy-filled potential of existence in God, and our response to this ignorance in ourselves and in others can only be one of understanding and compassion. The response to spiritual ignorance is not violence but love, and love can be awakened only by love. Jesus's commitment to his vision of life's abundant beauty and joy in God is evidenced in willingness to suffer and not to inflict suffering. Violence begets violence; it may arouse fear and command obedience but cannot overcome ignorance of God and awaken us to a compassionate and loving way of being. This was Jesus's purpose and hence his radical commitment to the way of non-violence.

The challenge of Jesus: The meaning of liberation

My perception of Jesus, however, not only affirms my Hindu understanding of authentic spirituality; in many important ways, Jesus also challenges and enriches my understanding. Jesus expresses his centeredness in God and his value for the world by being a vigorous spokesperson for the oppressed and the marginalized. He calls his own tradition to create an inclusive community where relationships are just and where our value for God is reflected in our value for each other. Jesus's representation of the liberated life as expressing itself in compassionate justice also challenges me intensely. It has inspired me to question prominent interpretations of Hinduism that represent liberation (*moksha*) as turning away from the world.

In my interpretation of the Hindu tradition, I highlight those important texts that characterize the liberated understanding as a way of seeing both God and the world.[20] These texts do not suggest that the world becomes unimportant in the vision of the liberated. Typical of such texts are the following from the Bhagavadgita (13:28; 18:20):

---

[20]   See Anantanand Rambachan, *The Advaita Worldview: God, World and Humanity* (Albany, NY: State University of New York Press, 2006) and *A Hindu Theology of Liberation: Not-Two Is Not One* (Albany, NY: State University of New York Press, 2015).

> One who sees the great Lord existing equally in all beings, the
> imperishable in the perishable, truly sees.
>
> That knowledge by which one sees one imperishable being in
> all beings, indivisible in the divisible is the highest.[21]

I understand these texts as inviting a way of seeing reality that does not
require negation of the world, but a celebration of its relationship with
God. Meaning and value are added, not taken from the world, when its
ontological unity and inseparable existence from God is affirmed. The
world exists both for the one who knows God and the one who does not
know God. The difference is that the knower of God understands the
world, despite its appearance of independent existence, to be dependent
on God. The world is seen with new eyes. Liberation enriches and does
not diminish the meaning of life in the world. Prominent among these
is the possibility of a deeper identity and affinity with all beings. This
is the outcome of understanding God to be the sole source and ground
of human selfhood. Isha Upanishad (6–7) relates this knowledge of the
unitive identity of God in all to freedom from hate, sorrow, and delusion:

> One who sees all beings in the self alone and the self in all beings,
> feels no hate by virtue of that understanding.
>
> For the seer of oneness, who knows all beings to be the self,
> where is delusion and sorrow?[22]

Liberation, in other words, should not alienate, isolate, or separate one
from the world and the community of beings, but awaken one to life's
unity in God.

In the Bhagavadgita, the discussion on the identity of God in all is
followed by a text (6:32) praising the liberated as one who owns the joy
and suffering of the other as one's own. On two occasions (5:25; 12:4),
the text employs the expression, "delighting in the well-being of all", to
describe the attitude of the liberated in relation to others. Liberation is

---

[21] Winthrop Sargeant (tr.), *Shri Bhagavad Gita* (Albany, NY: State University
of New York Press, 1930). My translation.

[22] My translation.

equated with an empathetic way of being. Seeing the suffering of another as one's own, however, becomes meaningless if this insight does not motivate compassionate action. What the Hindu tradition needs is a more expansive understanding of suffering and liberation. We cannot ignore the suffering of human beings when they lack opportunities to attain the necessities for dignified and decent living or when suffering is inflicted through oppression and injustice based on gender, caste, or race. Jesus is an insistent reminder of this necessity.

Questioning Jesus

I have spoken of my perception of Jesus as both affirming and challenging my understanding of what it means to be religious. Finally, I want to comment on the fact that my perception of Jesus also leaves me questioning. The questioning has to do with the absolute claims that are made by many Christians for Jesus on the basis of the biblical texts representing Jesus as the exclusive way to God and salvation (e.g. John 3:16,18; Acts 4:11–12; 1 Timothy 2:3–6; Hebrews 10:9–10). I am aware of some of the controversies of New Testament exegesis, including, for example, the contending images of Jesus in the Synoptic Gospels (Matthew, Mark, and Luke) and the Gospel of John and the claim that the latter, perhaps more than the other writers, is interpretative and expresses the faith of the early Church about the identity of Jesus. The outcome of such exegetical controversies on the relation between Christian claims and those of other religions remains open and the words of John, as an apostolic writer, ought to be taken seriously.

My questioning in relation to Christian exclusive claims for Jesus must be seen in relation to the deeply rooted Hindu view that divine self-revelation is not limited even to the boundaries of Hinduism. The argument that God revealed Godself fully and finally in one specific place and time compromises, from the Hindu viewpoint, the freedom and infinity of God. The Bhagavadgita (4:11), in a well-known verse, "Howsoever people approach me, so do I accept them; for the paths people take from every side are mine", suggests that divine self-revelation adapts itself to the diversity of humanity and that God responds appropriately to the yearning of the human being wherever and in whatever diverse forms this may be expressed. With rare exceptions, Hindus do not question the validity of Christianity as a way of religious fulfilment. The central difficulty for us is consistently with the Christian claim to be the only true way and the proselytizing monologue that this claim so often engenders.

Jesus's profound impact on me sits in unresolved tension with interpretations that appear all too often as arrogant and intolerant. I struggle with the fact that the Jesus I know is mediated through the lives of Christian friends and the teaching of institutions. At the same time, I must discern among interpreters and institutional doctrines and exercise a certain freedom, with all of its difficulties, in my effort at understanding Jesus. On the basis of the images of Jesus that emerge from the apostolic witnesses, we can surely speculate on whether the exclusive claims are consistent with the character of the person that is so eloquent in the texts. Let me cite Vivekananda from a lecture delivered in 1900 in Los Angeles:

> Suppose Jesus of Nazareth was teaching, and a man came and told him, "What you teach is beautiful. I believe that it is the way to perfection, and I am ready to follow it; but I do not care to worship you as the only begotten Son of God." "Very well, brother, follow the ideal and advance in your own way. I do not care whether you give me the credit for the teaching or not. I am not a shopkeeper. I do not trade in religion. I only teach truth and truth is nobody's property ... Truth is God Himself ..."

Vivekananda continued eloquently in depicting the humility and compassion of Jesus:

> What did he care if there was one man in the world that remembered him or not? He had to deliver his message and he gave it. And if he had twenty thousand lives, he would give them all up for the poorest man in the world. If he had to be tortured millions of times for a million despised Samaritans, and if for each of them the sacrifice of his own life was the only condition of salvation, he would have given his life. And all this without

wishing to have his name known even to a single person. Quiet, unknown, silent would he work ... [23]

Jesus's gaze as *Darshan*

My chapter is titled "Jesus Christ Under Hindu Gaze". From a Hindu perspective, however, it would be more appropriately called "A Hindu *Darshan* of Jesus". *Darshan* is the Sanskrit term that is used for the seeing of that which is sacred. We use it to describe our seeing of someone or something that has profound religious meaning and significance. *Darshan* is perception that awakens us to the reality of God. It is the experience of seeing and being seen by God. My *darshan* of Jesus, who is so radically God-centred, has enabled me, I believe, to see God more clearly and to be more attentive to the divine in our midst. At the same time, Jesus-*darshan* challenges me and enables me to see my own tradition in a new critical light. I embrace enthusiastically its vision of the world as divine celebration, in which we participate by seeing God in all through lives of compassion and justice. Jesus-*darshan*, at the same time, makes me aware of the exploitative and oppressive structures that alienate human beings from each other and from nature, and that often find religious justification. By seeing Jesus, I hope that I see more clearly those within and outside my own tradition who feel despised, rejected, and stripped of dignity.

The different Hindu religious traditions are also referred to as *darshans* (literally, ways of seeing). The use of this term suggests the limits of all ways of knowing and seeing, since these different ways express our temporal, spatial, and cultural locations as well as our identities, individually and as members of groups. Plurality, religious and otherwise, in other words, is a natural expression of the human condition and needs to be accepted as such. *Darshan* does not invalidate our ways of seeing but helps us to be both aware of our natural limits and open to learning from other *darshans*, within and outside of the Hindu tradition.

---

[23]   CW4, pp. 150–1.

6

A Buddha from Nazareth? Buddhist Interpretations of Jesus

Mathias Schneider

This chapter presents a brief overview of Buddhist interpretations of Jesus. During the history of Buddhist–Christian encounter, Buddhists from all major strands of their tradition have used different strategies either to polemicize against Jesus or to integrate him into their own doctrinal framework. The result is a broad spectrum of interpretations ranging from his demonization to his appreciation as a Bodhisattva or a Buddha. However, I will argue that this plurality of views was significantly shaped by external influences, most importantly the quality of historical Buddhist–Christian encounter and the interpreters' sociocultural and political contexts. Finally, I will discuss Christian responses to Christological challenges raised by Buddhist interpretations, reflecting on further avenues for a Buddhist–Christian Christology.

One of the greatest challenges of contemporary Christian theology is reflection on Christology in the context of religious plurality. In the past, Christian theologians have mostly reflected on other religious traditions exclusively from the perspective of their own. Furthermore, Christian encounters with religious Others were often conceived as missionary one-way roads, treating them as objects that had to be evangelized—and finally silenced. In recent decades, however, theological isolationism has begun to crumble. In the wake of interreligious dialogue and its reflection in academic disciplines, such as Intercultural and Interreligious/ Comparative Theology, Christian theologians are not only becoming increasingly aware of other religious traditions as valuable resources for theological growth. They are also beginning to take into account "the images of Christ, Christians, and Christianity that non-Christians have and use", and "to listen very carefully to what members of these communities have said and are saying about them".[1]

Reflection on Buddhist interpretations of Jesus is an important part of this growing theological mutuality. Throughout the global history of Buddhist–Christian encounter,[2] interpreters from all major strands of the Buddhist tradition, including Theravāda, Mahāyāna and Vajrayāna, from both Asia and the West have developed a large number of highly diverse portrayals of Jesus, which constitute a broad spectrum ranging from his demonization to his appreciation as a Bodhisattva or a Buddha.[3]

Buddhist–Christian hermeneutics

Before exploring the spectrum of Buddhist interpretations of Jesus, I will address some hermeneutical issues. First, Buddhist interpreters do not view Jesus in the framework of Christian concepts, but depict him in their own Buddhological categories. Second, Buddhist interpreters do not apply their doctrinal categories to Jesus in a vacuum, but are strongly influenced by various non-doctrinal factors of their respective contexts.

With his differentiation between "hetero-" and "auto-interpretation", Piet Schoonenberg has provided a hermeneutical framework to take into account the complex entanglements between doctrine and context: a *hetero-interpretation* is an external interpretation of a "reality—be it a person, community, tradition or institution—that is also interpreting

---

[1]   Paul Griffiths, "Introduction", in idem (ed.), *Christianity Through Non-Christian Eyes* (Maryknoll, NY: Orbis Books, 1990), pp. 1–11, here p. 3.

[2]   For an overview, see Michael von Brück and Whalen Lai, *Christianity and Buddhism: A Multicultural History of Their Dialogue* (Maryknoll, NY: Orbis Books, 2001).

[3]   I have treated the topic at large in Mathias Schneider, *Buddhistische Interpretationen Jesu: Eine religionshistorische und theologische Studie*, Beiträge zu einer Theologie der Religionen 26 (Zurich: TVZ, 2023).

itself", the latter being the *auto-interpretation* or self-understanding of that person, community, etc.[4] Hetero-interpretations are influenced by internal and external factors. *Internal factors* include an interpreter's own auto-interpretation and other doctrinal, ideological or hermeneutical presuppositions. Besides sociocultural and biographical contexts, one of the most important *external factors* is the quality of Buddhist–Christian encounter. Elizabeth Harris and Donald Lopez have summarized a mechanism describing the impact of historical encounter on doctrinal evaluations of Jesus: "when courtesy towards Buddhism was shown, courtesy was returned; when contempt was shown, defensive measures were taken to protect Buddhism from threat".[5] Or, applied to the figure of Jesus, "his estimation ris[es] in reverse proportion to the degree to which Buddhist authors felt threatened by his followers".[6] Thus, to some extent, Buddhist interpretations of Jesus are a mirror of the variegated history of Buddhist–Christian encounter.

Under the impact of internal and external factors, Buddhist interpreters choose doctrinal concepts and images from their own tradition to construct their hetero-interpretations of Jesus, implicitly or explicitly addressing one or more Christian auto-interpretations. At this point, one could raise a fundamental concern: does not every hetero-interpretation

---

4   Piet Schoonenberg, "Versuch einer christlich-theologischen Sicht des Hinduismus", in Gerhard Oberhammer (ed.), *Offenbarung, geistige Realität des Menschen: Arbeitsdokumentation eines Symposiums zum Offenbarungsbegriff in Indien*, Publications of the De Nobili Research Library 2 (Vienna: Sammlung De Nobili, 1974), pp. 171–87, here p. 172 (my translation).

5   Elizabeth Harris, "The Impact of Colonialism on Theravāda Buddhist–Christian Relations: An Overview", in Hans-Peter Grosshans, Samuel Ngun Ling and Perry Schmidt-Leukel (eds), *Buddhist and Christian Attitudes to Religious Diversity* (Yangon: Ling's Family Publication, 2017), pp. 183–207, here p. 188.

6   Donald Lopez, "Jesus in Buddhism: Closing Reflection", in Gregory A. Barker and Stephen E. Gregg (eds), *Jesus Beyond Christianity: The Classic Texts* (Oxford and New York: Oxford University Press, 2010), pp. 263–71, here p. 271.

constitute an illegitimate appropriation of the religious Other? If this were the case, any Buddhist hetero-interpretation could be regarded as an inclusivist takeover. However, two different meanings of inclusivism need to be distinguished.[7] On the one hand, *hermeneutical* inclusivism, i.e. starting to interpret the Other from the perspective of one's own religious tradition, is more or less unavoidable. *Theological* inclusivism, on the other hand, goes a step further by claiming an actual superiority of one's own hetero-interpretation or tradition against the Other's auto-interpretation. Therefore, interpreting Jesus from a Buddhist perspective (*hermeneutical* inclusivism) does not necessarily entail his theological subordination (*theological* inclusivism), because the Buddhological assessment of Jesus depends on the choice of specific doctrinal categories used for his interpretation—which are, in turn, influenced by historical Buddhist–Christian encounter. The result is a highly diverse spectrum of Buddhist hetero-interpretations of Jesus, ranging from his *exclusivist* demonization as a son of an evil deity, his *inclusivist* subordination as a seeker of enlightenment, to his *pluralist* appreciation as someone on a par with Gautama Buddha—a Buddha from Nazareth, as it were. In what follows, I will illustrate this spectrum with selected case studies centred on three Christological topics: the teachings of Jesus, the incarnation and the crucifixion.

Buddhist interpretations of Jesus

(1) Teachings of Jesus: *avidyā* or *upāya*?

Doctrinal and hermeneutical presuppositions
For many Buddhist interpreters, the teachings of Jesus provide a hermeneutical starting point to evaluate his salvific efficacy. According to traditional Buddhology, a fully enlightened Buddha (*samyaksaṃbuddha*) has discovered the timeless, ineffable cosmic truth, which he transmits

---

[7]   On the following distinction, see Reinhold Bernhardt, *Jesus Christus—Repräsentant Gottes: Christologie im Kontext der Religionstheologie*, Beiträge zu einer Theologie der Religionen 23 (Zurich: TVZ, 2021), p. 60.

to his followers in the form of his teachings. Both truth and teaching are known under the polysemantic term *dharma* and constitute the antidote to suffering (*duḥkha*) and the path to awakening (*bodhi*). The teaching of every Buddha contains the Four Noble Truths, including the Noble Eightfold Path (*āryāṣṭāṅgamārga*). Traditionally, its eight members[8] are organized into three interdependent "trainings" (*triśikṣā*): wisdom (*prajñā*), morality (*śīla*), and concentration/meditation (*samādhi*). According to a common Buddhist hermeneutics of religious diversity, non-Buddhist teachings can be considered salvific to the degree they contain the Eightfold Path (hereafter the "path criterion").[9] Therefore, Buddhist interpreters examine the teachings of Jesus whether they contain wisdom, morality and concentration, and if so, to what degree.

Jesus as a deluded deceiver
Negative interpretations of Jesus and his teachings predominantly developed in the context of colonialism and Christian mission. In a climate of Buddhist–Christian hostility, most Buddhists could not detect any element of the Eightfold Path in the teachings of Jesus as propagated by the missionaries. Instead, for many interpreters of the colonial period, Christian mission and European imperialism formed "a public and unholy alliance".[10] This becomes especially clear in the Theravāda Buddhist context of Sri Lanka, a country colonized by various European powers from the sixteenth to the twentieth century. Reviewing a history of hostile Buddhist–Christian debates, Buddhist reformer and fervent anti-Christian polemicist Anagārika Dharmapāla (1864–1933)

---

8   Right view, intention, speech, action, livelihood, effort, mindfulness, and concentration.

9   See Lily de Silva, "The Buddha, the Eightfold Path and the Other Religions", in Perry Schmidt-Leukel (ed.), *Buddhism and Religious Diversity, Vol. IV: Religious Pluralism* (Abingdon and New York: Routledge, 2013), pp. 117–29, here pp. 123–4. The canonical foundation for this view is *Dīgha Nikāya* 16.5.27, in Maurice Walshe (tr.), *The Long Discourses of the Buddha: A Translation of the Dīgha Nikāya* (Somerville, MA: Wisdom Publications, 1995), p. 268.

10   Brück and Lai, *Christianity and Buddhism*, p. 110.

accused Christianity of being "a political camouflage" whose "weapons are the Bible, barrels of whisky and bullets".[11] For Dharmapāla, however, the hidden political agenda of Christianity was no colonial invention, but could be traced back to its earliest days, when Jesus "promised" the "few illiterate fishermen of Galilee" power over Israel.[12]

A similar connection, albeit with a stronger demonizing tendency, was drawn by the earlier Sinhalese folk tale of the *Carpenter-Heretic* written down in 1762.[13] Under Portuguese rule (1506–1650s), Christian mission in Sri Lanka was directed against Buddhism and thus against an important part of Sri Lankan culture.[14] The narrative reflects this traumatic experience by demonizing Jesus as a son and *avatāra* or incarnation of Māra, an evil deity (*deva*) and antagonist of the Buddha. As an instrument of Māra, Jesus is sent to Sri Lanka, violates Buddhist ethical precepts and spreads false teachings in order to lead the populace astray from the Buddhist path of salvation. Just like the missionaries and their activities, Jesus and his teachings were perceived as an anti-Buddhist, diabolical attack concocted by Māra that had to be repelled.

Jesus as a teacher of morality

During the twentieth century, changing historical circumstances gradually gave way to dialogical openings between Buddhists and Christians. Therefore, many Buddhists did not perceive Christians as a threat anymore. Perceiving Christianity in a more positive light also led

---

[11] Quotes from Dharmapāla's writings are taken from the anthology of Ananda Guruge (ed.), *Return to Righteousness: A Collection of Speeches, Essays and Letters of the Anagarika Dharmapala* (Colombo: The Government Press, 1965); here, op. cit., p. 439.

[12] Guruge (ed.), *Return*, p. 475.

[13] For a translation, see Richard Fox Young and G. S. B. Senanayaka, *The Carpenter-Heretic: A Collection of Buddhist Stories about Christianity from 18th-Century Sri Lanka* (Colombo: Karunaratne & Sons Ltd, 1998), pp. 79–93.

[14] For historical overviews of regional Buddhist–Christian encounters described in this chapter, see Perry Schmidt-Leukel (ed.), *Buddhist–Christian Relations in Asia* (St Ottilien: EOS, 2017).

to a discovery of similarities between the teachings of Jesus and Gautama, resulting in a more positive evaluation of the former in terms of the path criterion.

Regarding the second "training" (śikṣā) of the Eightfold Path, morality (śīla), interpreters from all strands of the Buddhist tradition have generally appreciated the Sermon on the Mount as deeply akin to Buddhist ethics. In postcolonial Sri Lanka, Theravāda Buddhist Lily de Silva (1928–2015) highlighted the commandment of Jesus to love one's enemies (Matthew 5:44) and its application by forgiving his tormentors on the cross (Luke 23:34) as proof that he realized "the very fountain of all Buddhist virtues", compassion (karuṇā) and loving-kindness (maitrī), "to the highest possible level".[15] She also discerned significant aspects of the third training, concentration (samādhi), in the miracles of Jesus, which she interpreted as magical abilities (ṛddhividhi), traditionally regarded as products of an advanced meditative practice.[16]

However, for Lily de Silva and many other interpreters, Jesus's teaching of a personal creator god constitutes the major barrier for the discernment of the first training, wisdom (prajñā).[17] Most strands of Buddhist tradition have rejected the idea of a creator god with a broad arsenal of cosmological, ethical, soteriological, and logical arguments.[18] In the eyes of Buddhist critics, Jesus's call for faith in the existence of such a deity is thus both incompatible with the wisdom of a Buddha and a vivid demonstration of his own ignorance (avidyā). From the perspective of the path criterion, therefore, Lily de Silva's portrayal leads to an inclusivist subordination of Jesus as a still unenlightened, but nonetheless morally advanced teacher, below Gautama, who has perfected all three trainings of the Path.

---

[15] Lily de Silva, *The Buddha and Christ as Religious Teachers*, The Wheel Publication 380 (Kandy: Buddhist Publication Society, 1992), pp. 6–7, see also op. cit., p. 27.

[16] See Silva, *Buddha and Christ*, p. 5.

[17] See Silva, "The Buddha", p. 122.

[18] See Perry Schmidt-Leukel (ed.), *Buddhism, Christianity and the Question of Creation: Karmic or Divine?* (Aldershot and Burlington, VT: Ashgate, 2006).

Jesus as a teacher of skilful means

Not only for Theravāda but also for Mahāyāna interpreters, the path criterion has constituted an important hermeneutical tool. However, different doctrinal prerequisites like the concept of the two truths (*satyadvaya*) and the doctrine of skilful means (*upāyakauśalya*, short *upāya*) have allowed Mahāyāna interpreters a greater hermeneutical flexibility in their assessment of the theist teaching of Jesus. According to the *upāya* doctrine, Buddhas and advanced Bodhisattvas employ various teachings suited to the different needs and capacities of beings as a pedagogical means to guide them towards the realization of the ineffable, ultimate truth, which transcends these teachings. Related to Christology, the theist teaching of Jesus would then serve as a conceptual, penultimate "pointer" towards the ineffable, trans-conceptual ultimate reality.

This hermeneutical framework has been applied in inclusivist and pluralist ways. For the Japanese Zen missionary D. T. Suzuki (1870–1966), Jesus only *appears* to be marred by ignorance. Interpreted in his inclusivist framework of a "hidden Buddhist teleology", Jesus is an enlightened teacher in disguise, an "anonymous Buddhist"[19] deliberately utilizing preliminary teachings to prepare his followers for the *buddhadharma*, the actual higher (Buddhist) truth behind theism.[20] In several cases, an application of *upāya* hermeneutics is also combined with theological criticism. Masao Abe (1915–2006), for example, a representative of the Zen branch of the Kyōto School, attested to Christians a frequent confusion of their personal concepts of ultimate reality with the trans-conceptual ultimate reality itself, leading to the ultimate's reification and spiritually harmful clinging (*upādāna*) to its non-ultimate conceptualizations.[21]

---

[19] Both terms from Kristin Kiblinger, "Identifying Inclusivism in Buddhist Contexts", *Contemporary Buddhism* 4:1 (2003), pp. 79–97, here p. 88.

[20] See D. T. Suzuki, *Outlines of Mahâyâna Buddhism* (London: Luzac & Company, 1907), pp. 259, 275.

[21] See Masao Abe, "God, Emptiness, and the True Self", *The Eastern Buddhist, New Series* 2:2 (1969), pp. 15–30, here p. 23.

However, for the Vietnamese monk Thich Nhat Hanh (1926–2022), the danger to "confuse the means and the end, . . . the finger pointing to the moon and the moon" is a constant challenge for Christians and Buddhists alike.[22] In the teachings of Jesus and Gautama, he discerned the means to avoid this danger in culturally different, but functionally equivalent expressions: the teaching of mindfulness as the way to awaken to the true nature of reality.[23] In a similar way, Thai Theravāda reformer Bhikkhu Buddhadāsa (1906–93) severed the purported connection between theism and attachment with his hermeneutics of the two languages.[24] In this rather idiosyncratic interpretation of the two truths (*satyadvaya*), ultimate (*paramārtha*) and conventional (*saṃvṛti*) truth, Buddhadāsa identified two levels of meaning in religious language: spiritual ("*dhamma* language") and mundane ("everyday language"). Interpreted in *dhamma* language, the personal concept "God" and the impersonal concept "*dharma*" (Pāli *dhamma*) refer to the same unconditioned reality, because for Buddhadāsa, both guide practitioners to the realization of ultimate truth, manifested in a selfless (and thus liberated) mind.[25] Furthermore, if everybody "who can lead the world to perfect understanding" of this truth is a Buddha,[26] Buddhadāsa sees no obstacles to rank Jesus on a par with Gautama.[27] From this pluralist perspective, he can recommend the former's teachings, "[e]ven the short

---

[22]   Thich Nhat Hanh, *Living Buddha, Living Christ* (New York: Riverhead Books, 1995, reprinted 2007), pp. 54–5.

[23]   See Mathias Schneider, "Mindfulness, Buddha-Nature, and the Holy Spirit: On Thich Nhat Hanh's Interpretation of Christianity", *Buddhist–Christian Studies* 41 (2021), pp. 279–93.

[24]   See Perry Schmidt-Leukel, *Religious Pluralism and Interreligious Theology: The Gifford Lectures—an Extended Edition* (Maryknoll, NY: Orbis Books, 2017), pp. 80–1.

[25]   See Bhikkhu Buddhadāsa, *Christianity and Buddhism: Sinclaire Thompson Memorial Lecture, Fifth Series* (Bangkok: Karn Pim Pranakorn Partnership, 1967), pp. 3–10, 24–5, 43, 69–76.

[26]   Buddhadāsa, *Christianity and Buddhism*, p. 106.

[27]   See Buddhadāsa, *Christianity and Buddhism*, pp. 104–7.

message as contained in the few pages of the Sermon on the Mount", as "far more than enough and complete for practice to attain emancipation".[28]

(2) Incarnation: Son of Māra or *nirmāṇakāya*?

Doctrinal and hermeneutical presuppositions

In contrast to many Jewish or Muslim voices in dialogues on Christology,[29] most Buddhist interpreters have not denied the general idea of incarnation, i.e. a human being embodying a transcendent source. As José Cabezón points out, the reasons for this are functionally equivalent categories in their own tradition: the Buddhas and Bodhisattvas.[30]

However, Buddhist traditions differ in their conceptualizations of Buddhological equivalents. From a Theravāda Buddhist perspective, although the Buddha is revered as an embodiment of ultimate truth (*dharma*)[31] and the existence of many Buddhas is in principle acknowledged, traditional sources claim "that in each world system there cannot be more than one full Buddha at the same time".[32] In Mahāyāna and Vajrayāna Buddhism, however, two doctrines have sometimes led to a relativization of this restriction.[33] The first is the doctrine of the three Buddha bodies/realities (*trikāya*): the formless ultimate reality (*dharmakāya*) is manifested in the form of supranatural, celestial Buddhas (*saṃbhogakāya*), which again manifest as the manifold "transformation bodies" (*nirmāṇakāya*) of worldly Buddhas and Bodhisattvas. The

---

[28] Buddhadāsa, *Christianity and Buddhism*, p. 29.

[29] See parts 1–2 in Barker and Gregg (eds), *Jesus Beyond Christianity*.

[30] See José Ignacio Cabezón, "A God, but Not a Savior", in Rita M. Gross and Terry C. Muck (eds), *Buddhist Talk about Jesus—Christians Talk about the Buddha* (New York and London: Continuum, 2000), pp. 17–31, here pp. 24–5. Possible exceptions would be modernist voices, who—contrary to important canonical sources—deny any transcendent (*lokottara*) characteristics of the Buddha.

[31] See *Dīgha Nikāya* 27.9, in Walshe (tr.), *The Long Discourses*, p. 409.

[32] Schmidt-Leukel, *Religious Pluralism*, p. 75.

[33] For a more detailed discussion, see Schmidt-Leukel, *Religious Pluralism*, pp. 74–89.

second is the doctrine of Buddha-nature (*tathāgatagarbha*): ultimate reality is present in every sentient being, enabling them to become Buddhas themselves and to embody ultimate reality in the world. Thus, by drawing on one or both of these Buddhological doctrines, some Mahāyāna and Vajrayāna interpreters (and some Theravādins influenced by Mahāyāna Buddhism[34]) could also regard non-Buddhist teachers like Jesus as a manifestation of the *dharma*.

However, as the following examples from colonial contexts demonstrate, the mere existence of functional equivalents does not imply that all Buddhist interpreters have actually seen Jesus as an incarnation or accepted its Christian auto-interpretations without criticism.

Christology as an absurdity

In the wake of colonial Buddhist–Christian confrontations, Buddhist interpreters employed three main strategies in their polemical attacks on the idea of Jesus as an incarnation. First, some identified the transcendent source of Jesus with the evil *deva* Māra. In this respect, the tale of the *Carpenter-Heretic* presents an ironic twist: the missionaries' portrayal of Jesus as the son of a god fulfilling his father's plans is not denied—but this god is Māra, the lord of evil.

Second, Buddhist anti-theist criticism cast its shadow not only on Jesus's teachings, but also on the idea of Jesus as the incarnation of a creator god, which could "be no more acceptable than the God-idea itself".[35] Drawing on anti-theist arguments, Anagārika Dharmapāla related the theist teaching of Jesus to the character of its teacher: in his eyes, "[c]ruelty and muddle-headedness go hand in hand with the creator

---

[34]   Such as Buddhadāsa or the German Buddhist nun Ayya Khema (1923–97), see Mathias Schneider, "Demonic or Divine? Theravāda Buddhist Interpretations of Jesus", *Buddhist–Christian Studies* 39 (2019), pp. 259–70, here pp. 263–6.

[35]   Perry Schmidt-Leukel, "Buddhist Perceptions of Jesus: Introductory Remarks", in idem (ed.), *Buddhist Perceptions of Jesus: Papers of the Third Conference of the European Network of Buddhist–Christian Studies (St Ottilien 1999)* (St Ottilien: EOS, 2001), pp. 8–30, here p. 28.

idea",[36] a relation he illustrates with his caricature of Jesus as a simple human being with an irrational and unstable character ridden by mental defilements (*kleśa*).[37]

Third, Buddhists have accused Christians of misunderstanding the phenomenon of incarnation. In response to anti-Buddhist polemics of Jesuit missionaries in seventeenth-century China, the scholar-monk Ouyi Zhixu (1599–1655) attacked the missionaries' exclusivist claim for incarnational uniqueness in Jesus—a claim also accompanied by a disparagement of the Buddhas and Bodhisattvas as an *imitatio diabolica* of Christology.[38] Following a counter-exclusivist strategy, Zhixu accused the missionaries of incompetently plagiarizing the *trikāya* doctrine. First, he ridiculed the Christians' awkward distortion of the formless ultimate reality as an anthropomorphic, celestial being. Second, by limiting the manifestations of the universal *dharmakāya* to one single *nirmāṇakāya* (Jesus), the Christians would fail to "reach the wonderful radiance of the billions of 'bodies' of transformations"[39] familiar to the Mahāyāna tradition. In his eyes, limiting the manifestations of the all-encompassing ultimate reality to one single historical instance revealed Christology as an incoherent absurdity—and as the real *imitatio diabolica*.[40] Buddhist criticism of the uniqueness of incarnation remains one of the most challenging issues even in later, more positive Buddhist–Christian dialogues on Christology.

Jesus as a manifestation of ultimate reality
In the course of Buddhist–Christian encounter, various factors led to more positive Buddhist views on Jesus as an incarnation, for example the gradual emergence of dialogue initiatives in the nineteenth and twentieth

---

[36]   Guruge (ed.), *Return*, p. 419.

[37]   See Guruge (ed.), *Return*, pp. 439–42.

[38]   See Iso Kern, *Buddhistische Kritik am Christentum im China des 17. Jahrhunderts*, Schweizer Asiatische Studien 11 (Bern: Peter Lang, 1992), pp. 231, 260–1.

[39]   Kern, *Buddhistische Kritik*, p. 229, passage translated in Barker and Gregg (eds), *Jesus Beyond Christianity*, p. 230.

[40]   See Kern, *Buddhistische Kritik*, pp. 216–17.

centuries, or, as in the case of Tibet, the absence of colonialism.[41] In the case of appreciative Buddhist hetero-interpretations of the incarnation, two hermeneutical principles become visible. First, a necessary condition for regarding Jesus as an embodiment of ultimate reality is the recognition of qualities in his person, work, and teachings traditionally associated with Buddhahood, most significantly compassion (*karuṇā*) and wisdom (*prajñā*). As a case in point, the Fourteenth Dalai Lama's acceptance of Jesus as one of the "great beings who have infinite compassion toward all sentient beings" is the basis for appreciating him as "either a fully enlightened being or a bodhisattva of a very high spiritual realization".[42] Here, the Dalai Lama suspends a final decision whether to regard Jesus as a fully enlightened *nirmāṇakāya* Buddha or a not yet fully enlightened Bodhisattva. Similar to previous examples, however, each option also hinges on the evaluation of his theist teaching. From the perspective of Mahāyāna Buddhology, the first option would entail the identification of Jesus as a worldly manifestation of the ultimate *dharmakāya* in the framework of *upāya* hermeneutics, who skilfully applies his theist teaching to lure beings towards Buddhahood. According to the second option, Jesus would be a Bodhisattva, a being (*sattva*) altruistically pursuing the path to awakening (*bodhi*) by gradually developing the perfections (*pāramitā*)[43] necessary for the realization of Buddhahood. In the Mahāyāna tradition, entering the Bodhisattva path (i.e. to strive for Buddhahood) became the spiritual objective for (ideally) all practitioners—not for selfish reasons, however, but because a Buddha has realized all perfections to the highest degree and is thus of the utmost benefit for all other beings. Thus, as an advanced Bodhisattva, Jesus would be an epitome of compassion (*karuṇā*), showing considerable progress on the Bodhisattva path. Nevertheless, due to his deficits in wisdom

---

[41] For a more detailed analysis, see Schneider, *Buddhistische Interpretationen*, pp. 389–97.

[42] Dalai Lama, *The Good Heart: A Buddhist Perspective on the Teachings of Jesus*, ed. Robert Kiely (Somerville, MA: Wisdom Publications, 2016), p. 81.

[43] A common list of six perfections includes giving (*dāna*), morality (*śīla*), patience (*kṣānti*), vigour (*virya*), concentration (*dhyāna*) and wisdom (*prajñā*).

(*prajñā*) reflected in his theist teaching, Jesus would still be on a lesser stage of realization than a fully enlightened Buddha (*samyaksaṃbuddha*).

However, not every hetero-interpretation of Jesus as a Bodhisattva necessarily entails an inclusivist subordination. Buddhist tradition has often blurred the doctrinal divide between Buddhas and Bodhisattvas, as in the case of supranatural Bodhisattvas like Mañjuśrī or Avalokiteśvara.[44] Thus, by parallelizing Jesus and Avalokiteśvara, the Bodhisattva of compassion, as "exactly the same", Tibetan Lama Thubten Yeshe (1935–84) did not subordinate Jesus under a *samyaksaṃbuddha*, but emphasized his nature as permeated by "complete selfless devotion in the service of others".[45]

Both examples also disclose a second hermeneutical principle. If Buddhist interpreters can recognize qualities of Buddhahood in Jesus, the question is not *whether* he is an incarnation of ultimate reality, but to *which degree*. This principle shows a structural parallel to the Christological distinction between "substantialist" and "non-substantialist" conceptions of incarnation.[46] According to *substantialist* interpretations, embodying the divine nature is an ontological feature particular to Jesus. *Non-substantialist* interpretations, in contrast, conceive the divine nature as a universal anthropological quality by stressing gradual or functional (or both) dimensions of incarnation. Understood *gradually*, "everyone incarnates or embodies the presence of God, in so far and to the degree that he or she resonates ... with" its presence "in his or her life".[47] From a *functionalist* angle, this person would be an effective mediator of the

---

[44] See Perry Schmidt-Leukel, "Christ as Bodhisattva: A Case of Reciprocal Illumination", in idem and Andreas Nehring (eds), *Interreligious Comparisons in Religious Studies and Theology: Comparison Revisited* (London and New York: Bloomsbury, 2016), pp. 204–19, here pp. 211–12.

[45] Thubten Yeshe, *Introduction to Tantra: The Transformation of Desire*, rev. ed. Jonathan Landaw (Somerville, MA: Wisdom Publications, 2001), p. 55.

[46] See Perry Schmidt-Leukel, *Grundkurs Fundamentaltheologie: Eine Einführung in die Grundfragen des christlichen Glaubens* (Munich: Don Bosco, 1999), pp. 213–22.

[47] Perry Schmidt-Leukel, "Buddha and Christ as Mediators of the Transcendent: A Christian Perspective", in idem (ed.), *Buddhism and Christianity in*

divine presence precisely because he or she has become fully transparent for it. Both approaches do not necessarily imply the uniqueness of incarnation.

From an analogous "non-substantialist" Buddhological perspective, Buddhist interpreters present a two-fold challenge to Christian "substantialist" interpretations. First, most Buddhists do not conceive the transcendent source of incarnation in personal, but in impersonal terms. However, for Japanese Shin Buddhist interpreters like John Yokota, this transpersonal ultimate may also adopt personal form as the Buddha Amida.[48] In any case, appreciative readings of the incarnation depend on whether Buddhists are ready to concede "that the Christian concept of God does not point to a transient deity . . . , but to a reality which is both radically transcendent and radically immanent".[49] Second, even appreciative Buddhist interpreters unanimously reject the idea of incarnational uniqueness, as illustrated by Thich Nhat Hanh's reading of the doctrine of the two natures. "As the child of Mary and Joseph, Jesus is the Son of Woman and Man. As someone animated by the energy of the Holy Spirit"—a conception Thich Nhat Hanh identifies with Buddha-nature[50]—Jesus "is the Son of God".[51] Although Jesus differs from ordinary people because of his complete realization of the indwelling Spirit/Buddha-nature, this difference is not substantial, but gradual: every being has the capacity to become a Buddha and to embody ultimate reality in the world, because "we are of the same reality as Jesus".[52]

Dialogue: The Gerald Weisfeld Lectures 2004 (London: SCM Press, 2005), pp. 151–75, here p. 169.

[48] See John Yokota, "Where Beyond Dialogue? Reconsiderations of a Buddhist Pluralist", in David Ray Griffin (ed.), *Deep Religious Pluralism* (Louisville, KY: Westminster John Knox Press, 2005), pp. 91–107. For further Shin Buddhist accounts, see Schneider, *Buddhistische Interpretationen*, pp. 241–67.

[49] Schmidt-Leukel, *Religious Pluralism*, p. 168.

[50] See Schneider, "Mindfulness".

[51] Nhat Hanh, *Living Buddha*, p. 36.

[52] Nhat Hanh, *Living Buddha*, p. 44.

In sum, Buddhist views on the incarnation present a serious challenge to Christians: how can Christology deal constructively with Buddhist calls for a "phenomenology of breakthroughs of ultimacy"?[53]

(3) Crucifixion: A suffering saviour?

Doctrinal and hermeneutical presuppositions

How do Buddhist interpreters deal with the Christian auto-interpretation of Jesus as a suffering saviour? During the history of Buddhist–Christian encounter, Buddhist responses have ranged from ridicule and irritation to appreciative recognition. However, this spectrum shows a common doctrinal undercurrent, which can be described with Schubert Ogden's distinction between "constitutive" and "representative" soteriologies. According to a *constitutive* approach, salvation is caused by a specific event (e.g. the crucifixion as an unrepeatable atoning sacrifice effecting forgiveness of sins or divine satisfaction), i.e. "the possibility of salvation is nothing until the event occurs". According to a *representative* approach, the event "serves to declare a possibility of salvation that already is as it is prior to the event's occurring to declare it",[54] e.g. the "primordial and everlasting love of God".[55] This does not necessarily rule out other modes of representation.

In their own soteriological thought, Buddhist interpreters have mostly tended towards "representative" understandings of liberation: ultimate reality (*nirvāṇa, dharmakāya*, etc.) is already immanent in the mind (*citta*), e.g. as Buddha-nature, but needs to be actualized by following the spiritual path (*marga*) in order to "represent" it as an enlightened one. Therefore, most interpreters implicitly or explicitly reject a "constitutive" model of the crucifixion (with some important qualifications, see below)

---

[53] I borrow this term from Joseph O'Leary, "Toward a Buddhist Interpretation of Christian Truth", in Catherine Cornille (ed.), *Many Mansions? Multiple Religious Belonging and Christian Identity* (Eugene, OR: Wipf & Stock, 2002), pp. 29–43, here p. 34.

[54] Schubert Ogden, *Is There Only One True Religion or Are There Many?* (Dallas, TX: Southern Methodist University Press, 1992), p. 85.

[55] Ogden, *Is There*, p. 92.

on the ground of one or more of the following points of criticism. First, interpreters have criticized the often-implied restriction of salvation to Christians (exclusivism). Second, they have often recognized a neglect of active spiritual practice as a means to progress on the path towards liberation (gradual soteriologies). Third, they have objected to the role of the Christian God in atonement theories (theism). Fourth, some did not view the cross in positive or negative soteriological terms at all, but understood it as a contingent historical event (political interpretation).

Jesus as a criminal and the crucifixion as a failure
During the colonial period, Buddhist critics have raised two main lines of polemics. First, some interpreters saw the crucifixion as the just punishment of a subversive criminal. In the late "Christian century" (1549–1644) of Japan, anti-Buddhist hostility of evangelizing Christian missionaries and the fear of becoming colonized by European powers led to a ban against Christianity in 1614 and severe persecutions of Christians.[56] In this conflictual climate, missionaries were suspected of being subversive agents of colonial armies lying in wait for military invasion. Some Buddhist anti-Christian writings portrayed the Christians as diligent pupils of their master Jesus, who, as Buddhist polemicists did not fail to notice in the gospel narratives, was convicted of the attempt to usurp a royal title (e.g. Mark 15:26). In their eyes, just as the authorities of Jesus's time were justified in crucifying this rebellious criminal to prevent their domain from being seized by a dangerous subversive, the shogunate was justified in persecuting Christians in order to protect Buddhism and to preserve social and political order.[57]

Second, for some interpreters, Christian atonement theories expose God as morally repulsive and soteriologically incompetent. In Dharmapāla's eyes, "[a] god who loves to receive the blood of his own son

---

56   For an overview, see George Elison, *Deus Destroyed: The Image of Christianity in Early Modern Japan*, Harvard East Asian Monographs 141, 3rd edn (Cambridge, MA and London: Harvard University Press, 1991).

57   As, for example, in the ex-Jesuit Christovão Ferreira's *Kengiroku* ("Deceit Disclosed", 1636), translated in Elison, *Deus Destroyed*, pp. 295–318, here pp. 312–13.

to appease his own anger for the sins committed by some one [sic] else" could only be repelled as "monstrously diabolical".[58] Furthermore, in their counterattacks on exclusivist missionary soteriologies, Dharmapāla and Ouyi Zhixu could not detect any salvific effect in the sacrifice of the Son of God. Instead, it revealed God as an incompetent tyrant, because even after the supposedly redemptive sacrifice, the larger part of humanity (i.e. non-Christians) were still condemned to eternal punishment in hell.[59]

Jesus as a paradigm of selflessness and a self-sacrificing Bodhisattva

Not only Buddhist interpreters from colonial, but also from postcolonial contexts expressed their irritation against the sanguinary image of Jesus as a suffering saviour. One famous example is D. T. Suzuki, who constructed a stark dichotomy between the images of the meditating, serene Buddha and the crucified, agonized Christ—"a terrible sight" he could only "associat[e] . . . with the sadistic impulse of a physically affected brain".[60] However, this polemical and rather simplifying dichotomy should not remain the final Buddhist word on the crucifixion. Intensified dialogical encounters with Christians led some interpreters to a discovery of hitherto neglected aspects of the crucifixion, most importantly Jesus's voluntary self-surrender on the cross. Due to this hermeneutical shift, they could recognize the same selfless mind at work in the crucified one and in familiar figures from their own tradition, the Bodhisattvas.

In his reading of the *kenosis* motif of Philippians 2:5–11, Masao Abe portrayed the crucified Christ as a paradigm of selflessness and compassion. For Abe, the self-emptying (*kenotic*) pro-existence of Jesus with its culmination in his death on the cross symbolized the total overcoming of attachment to an illusionary ego-self (*ātmagraha*). The realization of selflessness (*anātman*) not only constitutes the core of a Bodhisattva's wisdom (*prajñā*), but also his capacity for non-discriminatory compassion (*karuṇā*) towards all beings, which Abe found symbolized in the resurrection. In this sense of a Bodhisattva's

---

58 Guruge (ed.), *Return*, p. 409.

59 See Guruge (ed.), *Return*, p. 409; Kern, *Buddhistische Kritik*, p. 230.

60 D. T. Suzuki, *Mysticism: Christian and Buddhist* (London and New York: Routledge, 2002), p. 119.

transparency for the dynamic interdependence of wisdom and compassion, Abe could accept Jesus as enlightened or "divine", precisely because in his *kenosis*, Jesus had refused clinging to a reified self or "divine nature" for the sake of the world.[61] In Abe's eyes, crucifixion and resurrection finally became a revelation of "absolute nothingness", the Kyōto School's reading of the Mahāyāna doctrine of emptiness (*śūnyatā*), i.e. the idea that reality is ultimately empty of any reified, intrinsic "self-nature" (*svabhāva*). However, this kenotic symbol of śūnyatā is not unique, but calls for an *imitatio Christi* in the life of every person.[62]

Another appreciative hetero-interpretation of the cross picks up where D. T. Suzuki left off. From a historical perspective, not only the Christian, but also the Buddhist tradition is familiar with "figures who are seen to voluntarily undergo suffering, even death, for the benefit of others":[63] the self-sacrificing Bodhisattvas. In a large number of traditional narratives and treatises, advanced Bodhisattvas are celebrated for voluntarily giving away limbs or their whole body (ātmabhāvaparityāga/*dehadāna*) if it is for the benefit of beings. In their ideal form, these (often very sanguinary) self-sacrifices are not only performed without any regret, but are also praised as the foremost sign of a Bodhisattva's "perfection of giving" (*dāna-pāramitā*), which requires a fully compassionate mind and the overcoming of attachment. Thus, for the Dalai Lama, the Christian auto-interpretation of Jesus as a suffering saviour undergoing excruciating pain for the sake of others is understandable in Buddhist terms as "a perfect example of . . . the Bodhisattva ideal".[64]

---

61   See Abe Masao, "Kenotic God and Dynamic Sunyata", in John B. Cobb, Jr and Christopher Ives (eds), *The Emptying God: A Buddhist–Jewish–Christian Conversation* (Maryknoll, NY: Orbis Books, 1990), pp. 3–65, here pp. 9–13, 32, 56.

62   See Abe, "Kenotic God", p. 11.

63   Paul Hedges, "The Body(sattva) on the Cross: A Comparative Theological Investigation of the Theology of the Cross in the Light of Chinese Mahayana Suffering Bodhisattvas", *Buddhist–Christian Studies* 36 (2016), pp. 133–48, here p. 141.

64   Dalai Lama, *Towards the True Kinship of Faiths: How the World's Religions Can Come Together* (London: Abacus, 2010), p. 57.

Yet, how does an interpretation of Jesus in terms of a self-sacrificing Bodhisattva deal with the idea of a suffering saviour *effecting* salvation? In his discussion of the self-immolation of the Vietnamese monk Thich Quang Duc in 1963 as a special form of Bodhisattva self-sacrifice, Thich Nhat Hanh suggested that the crucified Christ, like the self-sacrificing Bodhisattva, expresses not only boundless motivation to benefit others by their compassionate performance of suffering, but also to incite the "mind of awakening" (*bodhicitta*) in them.[65] In its initial form, *bodhicitta* denotes a Bodhisattva's altruistic aspiration to strive for Buddhahood for the welfare of all beings. Furthermore, according to Śāntideva (eighth century CE), *bodhicitta* is also a highly potent force of spiritual transformation, because, like medicine, it cures mental defilements (*kleśas*)[66]—and it is the foremost duty of a Bodhisattva to give this elixir to others, too. By applying the *bodhicitta* concept to Thich Nhat Hanh's reading of the cross, a cooperative model of salvation unfolds, combining aspects of "representative" and "constitutive" approaches. Ultimate reality is innate in the minds of sentient beings as the condition of the possibility of salvation, e.g. Buddha-nature (*representative*). However, because its real presence is shrouded by defilements, the unenlightened are in need of the "grace" of an external saviour. By performing selfless compassion to its utmost extreme, the Bodhisattva/Christ ignites the spark of *bodhicitta* in the minds of beings, thereby burning defilements and uncovering the ultimate's immanence (*constitutive*). This initial *bodhicitta*, in turn, can be cultivated by further imitation of the Bodhisattva's/Christ's attitude of self-surrendering compassion for the welfare of others, setting in motion a spiral of spiritual healing.

However, seen through a Buddhist lens, the suffering saviour Jesus changes his face: neither do interpreters assume the saviour's uniqueness, nor do they endorse the idea of divine installation of the sacrifice—it is a Bodhisattva's affair born out of the very fabric of the ultimate nirvāṇic ground of reality (compassion *plus* wisdom). Thus, as Paul Hedges

---

[65] See Thich Nhat Hanh, *Opening the Heart of the Cosmos: Insights on the Lotus Sutra* (Berkeley, CA: Parallax Press, 2003), pp. 113–14.

[66] See Śāntideva, *The Bodhicaryāvatāra*, tr. Kate Crosby and Andrew Skilton (Oxford and New York: Oxford University Press, 1995), p. 22 (3.29–31).

aptly puts it, Buddhist interpretations pose a challenge for widespread Christian soteriologies: "Can we imagine a bodhisattva on the cross?"[67]

A Buddha from Nazareth?

I will conclude this overview with a brief outlook on Christian receptions of Buddhist interpretations of Jesus. In recent times, Christian theologians from a broad confessional spectrum have responded to Buddhist voices. Compared to the general field of systematic theology, the number of explicit Christian reactions is small, but growing. From a theological angle, Buddhist interpretations of Jesus include a two-fold normative dimension. On the one hand, as demonstrated in the previous cases, even the most appreciative Buddhist portrayals contain implicit or explicit criticism of widespread Christian doctrinal tenets. On the other hand, Buddhist interpreters claim to have a correct—or simply a better—understanding of Jesus. Both dimensions constitute a theological challenge to Christians that deserves a differentiated and sincere evaluation.

However, not every Christian respondent has welcomed the challenge. In their apologetical rejections, some Christian voices are dismissive of Buddhist points of criticism without giving these points a closer theological scrutiny. Instead (and perhaps surprisingly), their main emphasis lies in the rebuttal of appreciative Buddhist portrayals of Jesus. These apologetical stances are, among others, informed by Christian superiority claims which assume that divine revelation is present in Christianity alone or at least in a uniquely superior form. From this view, appreciative Buddhist hetero-interpretations of Jesus threaten Christian superiority claims, because they imply comparability—which, in turn, implies (at least to a certain degree) the recognition of similarity, correspondence, or even congruence that may lead to a critical review of claims for the salvific uniqueness of Christianity and Jesus.[68] Thus, a frequent reaction consists in reinforcing Christian superiority claims,

---

[67]   Hedges, "The Body(sattva)", p. 143.

[68]   See Schneider, *Buddhistische Interpretationen*, p. 436.

for example by insisting on the uniqueness of incarnation in Jesus or by interpreting doctrinal differences as insurmountable. Furthermore, some apologists exhort their Christian colleagues to avoid the Christological application of non-Christian categories like "Buddha" or "Bodhisattva", because this kind of hermeneutical borrowing would inevitably result in a distortion of Christian identity.[69]

Whereas Christian apologists have perceived Buddhist hetero-interpretations as a threat and denied their theological value, other Christian voices do not insist on an exclusive "copyright" on Jesus. Instead, they welcome Buddhist perceptions as opportunities for constructive interreligious learning and even as valuable contributions to intra-Christian debates. Therefore, to a certain degree, they are also open for Buddhist points of criticism as outlined above.

By way of conclusion, I will briefly sketch some potential fields of comparative-theological transformation. First, Buddhist warnings of an absolutization of doctrinal concepts of ultimate reality fall on fertile ground. In the cases of Paul Knitter, Roger Haight and others, Buddhist voices have stimulated a rediscovery of often-neglected apophatic strands of Christian tradition. These contain their "own brand of non-duality"[70] that seriously takes into account the ineffability of the transcendent and provides resources for a fresh mystagogical, "upāyic" understanding of Christological concepts.[71]

Some Christians also feel confirmed in their own criticism of juridical–satisfactional atonement theories. In dialogue with the motif

---

[69] For a brief discussion of some of these arguments, see Mathias Schneider, "Who Owns Jesus? Reflections from Buddhist–Christian Dialogue on Christology", *Interreligious Insight* 20:2 (2022), pp. 36–43. For a more comprehensive overview of positive and negative Christian responses, see Schneider, *Buddhistische Interpretationen*, part IV.

[70] Paul Knitter and Roger Haight, *Jesus and Buddha: Friends in Conversation* (Maryknoll, NY: Orbis Books, 2015), p. 83.

[71] See John Hick, "Religion as 'Skilful Means': A Hint from Buddhism", *International Journal for Philosophy of Religion* 30:3 (1991), pp. 141–58. Reprinted in John Hick, *Disputed Questions in Theology and the Philosophy of Religion* (Basingstoke: Macmillan, 1993), pp. 119–36.

of the self-sacrificing Bodhisattva, they reclaim a "representative" understanding of the cross and emphasize the transformational function of the Christ as a spiritual healer.[72] As Joseph O'Leary puts it:

> Jesus draws on himself the violence generated by human greed and ambition, eloquently countering it in his death with an expression of forgiveness, compassion, humility, and love . . . . Jesus has a bodhisattva's insight into the bondage of his enemies to delusive passions . . . , rooted in a delusive idea of self, and he exerts educative compassion on their condition, to release them from suffering. Wherever the cross is made known, the same compassionate education is continued.[73]

However, Christians can also learn from Buddhist voices who have perceived the cross not as a symbol of compassion, but as a figurehead of colonial violence and missionary threat. In this way, negative interpretations of Jesus hold up a mirror to exclusivist Christologies. Consequently, some theologians transcend the aporia of exclusivism by not confining the phenomenon of incarnation to Jesus. If the same selfless, compassionate mind that Buddhists and Christians associate with a salvific "*immanence* of the transcendent"[74] can be experienced not only in Jesus, but also in the Buddhas and Bodhisattvas, Perry Schmidt-Leukel argues for a non-substantialist interpretation of incarnation that "seriously reckon[s] with the possibility . . . of several incarnations" or mediators of ultimate reality.[75] In that case, Buddhological and Christological categories would not describe incommensurable phenomena, but provide different yet complementary perspectives on a plurality of breakthroughs of ultimate reality.

These Christian impulses point towards an alternative approach to Christology as a collaborative, interreligious enterprise—a development

---

[72]   See Hedges, "The Body(sattva)", pp. 142–3.

[73]   O'Leary, "Toward", pp. 33–4.

[74]   Schmidt-Leukel, "Christ as Bodhisattva", p. 214 (italics in the original).

[75]   Schmidt-Leukel, "Buddha and Christ", p. 169.

that has already begun. So perhaps, the future might bring what Alfred North Whitehead (1861–1947) described in 1926:

> The Buddha gave his doctrine to enlighten the world: Christ gave his life. It is for Christians to discern the doctrine. Perhaps in the end the most valuable part of the doctrine of the Buddha is its interpretation of his life.[76]

---

[76] Alfred North Whitehead, *Religion in the Making: Lowell Lectures 1926* (Cambridge: Cambridge University Press, 1926; new impression, 1927), p. 45.

7

Liberating White Jesus: A Palestinian Liberation Theology Approach to Tackling Racism, Antisemitism, and Colonialism in Christology

Paul Hedges

This chapter uses Palestinian liberation theology alongside the work of Emmanuel Levinas and others to explore the antisemitic, racist, and imperial aspects of traditional High Christology. It is argued that the Christian tradition cannot escape structural antisemitism in its Christological formulations within what has become the mainstream tradition. It explores how the three aspects of antisemitism, racism, and imperialism have become bound together in Christology and the wider Christian tradition, before suggesting how we can help free a Jewish Palestinian prophet from the bondage of the "White Jesus" which, thinking with Levinas, entails us taking on a messianic identity to act to heal the world (tikkun olam). *Naim Stifan Ateek's arguments, including his critique of older liberation theological reliance on the Exodus narrative, are advanced to show how a Palestinian Liberation Theology may help us envisage this theologically. The chapter also offers theological reflection on how Lady Spirit may be leading us today.*

Jesus was Jewish and to think about him in High Christological terms is to be implicated in racism, antisemitism, and imperialism. That is a lot to say in one sentence. It may offend. Yet, it is an argument convincingly made elsewhere,[1] and one which I believe holds water. It forms a basis for this chapter. I will therefore cover that argument to begin the chapter, also offering an extension of it. Previously, I have used the argument to suggest the need for a revised Christology, and here I tread further along that path by considering how Palestinian liberation theology may help us rethink our Christological frames. Specifically, I will consider how Naim Stifan Ateek, a Palestinian liberation theologian and Anglican priest, has addressed the plight of his people and aspects of Christian thought to seek to liberate the "White Jesus". It may be noted that Ateek has been accused, unfairly and unjustly I believe, of being antisemitic. As such, bringing Palestinian Christian theology into alignment within an anti-antisemitic frame may seem fraught. Yet it is the tough questions which we must ask, and this may help us see things anew as we rethink Christology and messiahship beyond racist, imperialist, and antisemitic frames of reference.

This chapter consists of three main parts. First, what I term "Jesus, Racism, Antisemitism, and Imperialism" in which I survey and extend arguments about how racism, antisemitism, and imperialism have become part of how Christology (the Christian tradition) is structured and framed. The second part will discuss my previous arguments about how we need to rethink the person of Jesus by disassociating him from the "White Jesus" model, and how Emmanuel Levinas may help us rethink our concept of messiahship, entitled "An Argument Revisited: Beyond White Jesus". In the third section, "A Liberationist Palestinian and Anti-Antisemitic Christology", I introduce Ateek's arguments, including providing an introduction to Palestinian liberation theology and some themes within it, including its critique of older liberation theological reliance on the Exodus narrative. This will provide a frame for exploring a notion of what it means for us to act in the role of a "messiah" inspired by Jesus's example (why we must act as such is explored as we proceed). Finally, a very brief "Towards Further Exploration", rather than

---

[1]   See Paul Hedges, "White Jesus and Antisemitism: Toward an Antiracist and Decolonial Christology", *Current Dialogue* 72:5 (2020), pp. 777–96, which contains extended arguments and references related to the core claims that frame this chapter.

being—in any way—a conclusion to this conversation, will build upon the arguments to suggest how Lady Spirit may be leading us today.

Jesus, racism, antisemitism, and imperialism

I begin by outlining the argument that how we typically envisage Jesus, within High Christological formulations, is not simply antisemitic, but bound up in both racist and imperialist thinking. Within one chapter it is not possible to cover all aspects of this argument, for instance as regards Christianity's immersion within antisemitic tropes, discourse, and ideological frames; entire books are dedicated to this,[2] and, as such, the scope of the argument here relies upon this surrounding and wider literature set. Nevertheless, the basis of the argument may be set out here.

I begin with antisemitism, which has been a feature of the Christian tradition for almost as long as Christianity has existed, and still infects it in many ways today.[3] Without seeing the Newer Testament itself as antisemitic, it has been read and interpreted this way by later Christians who are divorced from what is essentially the intra-Jewish debates of its authors. While a number of passages have been important, three short texts have often been key: Matthew 27:25, "His blood be on us [Jews] and on our children"; John 8:44, "You [Jews] are from your father

---

[2]   The classic works are Rosemary Radford Ruether, *Faith and Fratricide: The Theological Roots of Anti-Semitism* (New York: Seabury, 1974), and James Parkes, *The Conflict of the Church and the Synagogue: A Study in the Origins of Antisemitism* (New York: Atheneum, 1977). Specific studies include James Carroll, *Constantine's Sword: The Church and the Jews* (Boston, MA: Houghton Mifflin, 2001), and Thomas Kaufmann, *Luther's Jews: A Journey into Anti-Semitism* (Oxford: Oxford University Press, 2017). For essay-length surveys, see Ronald Miller, "Judaism: Siblings in Strife", in Paul Hedges and Alan Race (eds), *Christian Approaches to Other Religions* (London: SCM Press, 2008), pp. 176–90, and Paul Hedges, *Religious Hatred: Prejudice, Islamophobia, and Antisemitism in Global Contexts* (London: Bloomsbury, 2021), pp. 51–66.

[3]   See Hedges, *Religious Hatred*, pp. 109–10.

the devil"; and John 20:19, "the doors of the house where the disciples had met were locked for fear of the Jews". Read into later tradition and literature of the Church Fathers—termed *Adversus Judaeos*—polemic against Jews and Judaism seeped into the very lifeblood of Christian thinking, both in the Greek East and the Latin West through figures such as Tertullian, John Chrysostom, and Augustine of Hippo. Ellen Charry suggests it entails a forgetting of Israel, with it being erased from how Christians think about G*d,[4] salvation, and the tradition they inherited/took over.[5] The antisemitism[6] of the Christian Church made the Shoah possible, something taken on board by mainstream churches post-Shoah as they have acknowledged their role in that genocide.[7] Yet, I would argue,

---

[4]   Writing G*d instead of God is a fairly recent custom in America. Many believe this to be a sign of respect, and the custom comes from an interpretation of the commandment in Deuteronomy 12:3–4 regarding the destruction of pagan altars. <https://reformjudaism.org/learning/answers-jewish-questions/why-do-some-jews-write-g-d-instead-god>, accessed 16 October 2023.

[5]   Ellen Charry, "Who Delivered Israel from Egypt?", *Theology Today* 74:3 (2017), pp. 263–74.

[6]   Some scholars argue that before the eighteenth or nineteenth centuries we see anti-Judaism, a Christian/religious hatred, with antisemitism appearing only with the racialized conception of Jews as Semites separated from the earlier religious foundations. But this distinction is not analytically accurate. First, aspects of older theological tropes are part of the modern conception, with the Enlightenment secularizing but maintaining them, and this feeds into the racialized hatred. Second, from around the fifteenth or sixteenth centuries, the Christian hatred of Jews was racialized via the blood lineage ideology of the Iberian Peninsula. While a twelfth-century Christian hatred of Jews differs from a twenty-first-century politicized anti-Israeli hatred of Jews, tropes are shared and a lineage of thinking binds them. I therefore argue that, while anachronistic before the nineteenth century (when the term antisemitism was coined), we simply refer to all forms of hatred of Jews as antisemitism. See Hedges, *Religious Hatred*, p. 5.

[7]   For a brief outline, see Victoria Barnett and Franklin Sherman, "Jews and Christians: The Unfolding Interfaith Relationship", *United States Holocaust Memorial Museum* (n.d.). See also the readings in note 2.

statements of regret, changes in language, attempts to embrace Jesus's Jewishness, and engagement in dialogue, as well as being seen as often inadequate if not inappropriate by Jews and Jewish groups,[8] also neglect a deeper problem—that of structural antisemitism.

Specifically in relation to Christological thinking, it can be noted that:

> to think a high Christology, to think in orthodox trinitarian forms about Jesus as affirmed in the Nicaean–Chalcedonian tradition, is to be implicated within the antisemitism of the authors and lineage that developed them ... [T]hese councils and debates came within a context that explicitly sought to divide Christianity's root and branch from its Jewish heritage as a triumphalist agenda of imperial Christianity.[9]

This is where it is useful to think through the lens of prejudice studies and anti-racist work. As work against racism began in the late twentieth century, a realization dawned that it was not adequate simply to be personally not racist. If I only stop at being non-discriminating myself, then I leave intact discriminatory ways of thinking, talking, and being within the wider society. Indeed, I may even not realize that structures exist within my society that culturally favour certain groups over others, or are shaped in ways that favour one group over another.[10] For instance, to take an unrelated example, it has been observed that, at least in the USA, the hospice movement has been predicated upon people consciously choosing less medicalized interventions in a context where highly medicalized interventions are readily available. But for people of colour, to whom highly medicalized interventions are not as readily available,

---

8   See Alana Vincent, "Convergence and Asymmetry: Observations on the Current State of Jewish-Christian Dialogue", *Interreligious Studies and Intercultural Theology* 4:2 (2020), pp. 201–23.

9   Hedges, "White Jesus and Antisemitism", p. 792.

10   See, for instance, Tendayi Achiume, "Beyond Prejudice: Structural Xenophobic Discrimination Against Refugees", *Georgetown Journal of International Law* 45:3, available at: <https://ssrn.com/abstract=2294557>, accessed 16 October 2023.

hospices seem to be just another way to deny them something which they already struggle to access and are often denied. A white, educated, middle-class expectation of advanced and life-prolonging medical interventions may underlie the hospice movement.[11] This fits within a context where we know that people of colour are routinely prescribed less pain relief medication because of an implicit assumption of doctors (who may be personally non-racist) that certain groups of people are more tolerant of pain, or they may misread culturally determined ways of expressing pain.[12]

Anti-racism campaigners have urged us, because of structures and implicit bias, to recognize that simply being personally not racist will not challenge deeper problems and inherent underlying systemic aspects of race discrimination and prejudice within both society and ourselves. When we turn to theology and ecclesial structures, therefore, simply seeing statements of regret about our past, or changing some surface wording, such as a liturgical formula, does not prompt interrogation of the deeper structural and implicit problems. If antisemitism is something that seems to come "naturally" from our texts—without realizing that we are reading a text of one group of Jews debating another group of Jews—then reading that "the Jews"[13] demanded Jesus's death may readily lead to the traditional charge of deicide. Again, Paul, who was a trained rabbinical thinker, was, as Jewishly informed scholars have told us, engaged in Midrash, or traditional Jewish exegesis and argumentation, in his epistles. Yet, when read as a Christian writer, we have seen Paul—or Saul of Tarsus—making a distinction between a Christian "religion of grace" and a Jewish "religion of law", which, apart from being

---

[11]   See Lucy Bregman, "Hospice: The Search for Better Dying", in Kathleen Garces-Foley (ed.), *Death and Religion in a Changing World*, 2nd edn (London: Routledge, 2022), pp. 205–25, 215.

[12]   See Carmen R. Green et al., "The Unequal Burden of Pain: Confronting Racial and Ethnic Disparities in Pain", *Pain Medicine* 4:3, pp. 277–94, <https://doi.org/10.1046/j.1526-4637.2003.03034.x>, accessed 16 October 2023.

[13]   On this term, see Hedges, *Religious Hatred*, p. 52.

anachronistic, fails to see how he was engaged in intra-Jewish debates.[14] It is hard to free ourselves from antisemitic tropes and traditions which have been embedded into our tradition. As the Church historian Jaroslav Pelikan noted long ago, while for the first-century followers of Jesus his Jewishness and being a rabbi was obvious, in the second century it was an embarrassment, and by the third had become obscure or simply incomprehensible.[15] In fact, much was shared between these twin traditions up until the fourth century, as textual scholars of these traditions tell us, and up until at least the early fourth century there are texts from each tradition which we have uncovered, and which may be either Jewish or Christian, yet without information outside of the texts themselves we cannot always tell which is which.[16] But, from the fourth century, the Christian tradition, in its transition to a new imperial formation, formalized a decisive split with Judaism that divorced Jesus from his Jewish roots in Christology as well as implementing a directly anti-Jewish ideological formation.[17]

Learning from prejudice studies, therefore, informs us that the deep structures of Christianity may be embedded in systemic antisemitism, and so simply saying we are not antisemitic ourselves is not enough. The way we read and engage the canon has become imbued with antisemitism. We are hard pressed to find a single foundational thinker and shaper of Christianity amongst the Church Fathers, or even later theologians, who is not habitually antisemitic. It is in the DNA of Christianity, and even

---

[14] See Miller, "Judaism", p. 188, n. 3, and Pamela Eisenbaum, *Paul Was Not a Christian: The Original Message of a Misunderstood Apostle* (New York: HarperOne, 2010).

[15] Jaroslav Pelikan, *Jesus Through the Centuries: His Place in the History of Culture* (New Haven, CT and London: Yale University Press, 1985).

[16] See Judith Lieu, *Neither Greek Nor Jew* (London: Bloomsbury, 2016), pp. 31–49, though some kind of break begins from the second century. See Hedges, *Religious Hatred*, p. 227, n. 10.

[17] In relation to Christology, see Hedges, "White Jesus and Antisemitism", pp. 785–6, 789, 792. See also: Carroll, *Constantine's Sword*, and Ruether, *Faith and Fratricide*, pp. 183–95.

what may seem to be sharing the Gospel may be antisemitic in ways we do not normally stop and see.[18]

This leads us to the imperialism within Christianity. Many writings portray Constantine as the man responsible for changing Christianity into something new. Embedded in a "great man" way of reading history, such simplistic arguments may make compelling narratives with a clear villain and an identifiable turning point, but they mask much more complex, nuanced, and intricate flows of changes, developments, and competing narratives. Yet, to speak of a Constantinian turn in Christian history is not entirely undue if we see it as marking not a single man's achievement but wider changes over time. Constantine in his role as emperor could exert a huge influence (but, of course, only lastingly significant in the light of his successors). By making a new Christian civil service in his capital as a loyal base to break the power of the old Roman aristocracy (almost certainly not because he was personally a Christian[19]), and in calling the first of what would be many councils to determine between what we have come to term orthodoxy and heresy, he set patterns in place.[20] As social studies have shown, the Jesus Movement appealed to the lower classes and to women in particular in its early decades, and remained somewhat marginal even if sizable by the early fourth century. Yet, with Constantine and then his successors Christianity

---

[18]   Hedges, *Religious Hatred*, p. 52.

[19]   While most histories repeat the well-worn trope that Constantine converted to Christianity following the sign of the cross (or Chi-Rho symbol) revealed before the Battle of the Milvian Bridge, Alistair Kee has offered a detailed and convincing argument that contemporary records dispute it was a Chi-Rho, while the emperor retained his patron as Apollo, and that even Eusebius was careful never to refer to him as a Christian while he lived (*Constantine Versus Christ: The Triumph of Ideology* (London: SCM Press, 1982)). Despite vitriolic reviews and offhand dismissal, I have yet to see a refutation of Kee's arguments.

[20]   On Christianity's change in Constantine's wake, see Kee, *Constantine Versus Christ*, and on the politics and social context, see Linda Woodhead, *An Introduction to Christianity* (Cambridge: Cambridge University Press, 2004), pp. 33–51.

became implicated fully in the imperial system. Art history shows us that the young, tunic-wearing peasant Jesus of catacomb art moves to become the King of the Universe, even in Roman military regalia, in the Constantinian wake. Likewise, the twinned connection with Judaism, as noted, becomes severed. After this, there is no confusion about whose texts are whose: theology becomes enshrined in the imperialist council system, and Jesus is ever more distanced from any connection with the man from Galilee.[21] Antisemitism and imperialism go hand-in-hand in defining the Creeds and formulas which we know.[22] From an anti-racist perspective, we must therefore ask what are the systemic structures built into Christianity.

We must take anti-antisemitism, anti-imperialism, and anti-racism as a package because all of these are entwined.[23] We have, for almost 2,000 years, read Jesus as not Jewish, as an imperial King of the Heavens, as divorced from his own milieu, and as repudiating Judaism in his very essence and being. This is not simply about a particular doctrine, a few liturgical phrases, or some "unfortunate" words that a figure such as Luther may have said,[24] but the embedded consciousness of a tradition. Its very structure and essence, seen in the words of almost every major thinker, and then implicitly built into the fabric of speaking, practice, and being, are infused with antisemitic and imperialist ideology. It is no coincidence that Jews were regularly killed in medieval Christendom during "Holy" Week—"holy" for whom, and what kind of "holiness"

---

[21]   This is not to ascribe the so-called "historical Jesus" to the "Christ of faith" change to this period, with Hellenistic influence occurring from the earliest days of the Jesus Movement; see Paul Hedges, *Understanding Religion: Theories and Methods for Studying Religiously Diverse Societies* (Oakland, CA: University of California Press, 2021), pp. 104–11.

[22]   See Hedges, "White Jesus and Antisemitism", pp. 784–9.

[23]   Frantz Fanon noted what he was told by his philosophy professor in Martinique: "Whenever you hear anyone abuse the Jews, pay attention, because he is talking about you." *Black Skin, White Masks*, tr. Charles Markmann (London: Pluto Press, [1952], 1986), p. 122.

[24]   See Hedges, "White Jesus and Antisemitism", pp. 784–5, 787–8.

is it that Christians believed that the supposed theological–liturgical highlight of their year was a time for the slaughter of innocents?[25]

Into this matrix, we may add one last element: the "White Jesus" of the title. A recognition of Jesus's Jewishness entails a further acknowledgement, especially when we realize, as recent studies have shown, that he was a teacher of the countryside and villages, that he was an Eastern Mediterranean peasant, a brown-skinned Palestinian (a term we return to below).[26] Here, we must turn to another facet of the argument, which focuses on "the 'white Jesus' of the Christian imagination"[27] and which relates not just to the fact that Jesus's Jewishness is erased but the predominant forms of Christian narrative and tradition within our globe today spread from within a Eurocentric worldview. That is to say, through the colonialism of the last few centuries, European culture and ideas have spread globally to become hegemonic, something true intellectually,[28] economically, and in terms of the cultural imagination. This has also meant that Eurocentric Christianities have become the dominant global norm, and with it their way that Jesus is thought and imagined.[29] Even when we seek to make Jesus, or Christianity, appear indigenous or take

---

[25] See David Nirenberg, *Anti-Judaism: The History of a Way of Thinking* (New York: W. W. Norton, 2013).

[26] On Jesus as non-white and how he may have looked: academically, see Joan Taylor, *What Did Jesus Look Like?* (London: T&T Clark, 2018). On Jesus's first-century Palestinian context, see John Dominic Crossan, *The Historical Jesus: The Life of a Mediterranean Jewish Peasant* (San Francisco, CA: HarperSanFrancisco, 1991).

[27] Hedges, "White Jesus and Antisemitism", p. 779.

[28] See Syed Farid Alatas, "Academic Dependency and the Global Division of Labour in the Social Sciences", *Current Sociology* 5:1 (2003), pp. 599–613.

[29] See e.g., Mercy Amba Oduyoye, "African Culture and the Gospel: Inculturation from an African Woman's Perspective", in Mercy Amba Oduyoye and Hendrik M. Vroom (eds), *One Gospel—Many Cultures: Case Studies and Reflections on Cross-Cultural Theology* (Amsterdam: Rodopi, 2003), pp. 39–62; Werner Ustorf, "The Cultural Origins of 'Intercultural Theology'", *Mission Studies* 25 (2008), pp. 229–51; and James Cone, *Black Theology and Black Power* (New York: Harper & Row, 1969).

on local flavour, it is through this lens as "inculturation is often focused not upon the Jewish Jesus, but upon the white Jesus".[30] As such:

> White Jesus is not simply the Jesus of a certain branch of the Caucasian peoples of the northwestern end of the Eurasian landmass but the image transported globally and enforced in conversion by the cross and the sword, such that one would not be surprised in entering a church in Argentina or Angola, Singapore or Swaziland to catch sight of a white Jesus.[31]

We are, of course, not simply talking about the colour of Jesus's skin here, but the structural way that Jesus is imagined and thought, and this continues with the now dominant US hegemonic power still perpetuating Eurocentric norms within theology, such that in "academic theology . . . the canon remains centred on a Euro-normative corpus; whether it is Barth, Tillich, Aquinas, Luther, Calvin, Hauerwas or Rahner, such white, Western writers remain the standard works. Non-Western theology, when it is included, remains a footnote as contextual theology."[32] Our Christological thinking is, today, therefore haunted not simply by an ancient legacy of imperialist antisemitic norms, but has become infused with several centuries of white, Western, colonialism. Critics have long pointed to this "Latin captivity of the Church",[33] and theologies against imperialism and colonialism have certainly arisen.[34] Yet, as I argue, a deeper structural issue arises within the Christian world. Just the week before writing this essay, I was directed to a work by an Asian theologian which focused on the need for Karl Barth in their context, a pattern repeated time after time, as certainly no Protestant Christian priest/

---

[30]   Hedges, "White Jesus and Antisemitism", p. 778.

[31]   Hedges, "White Jesus and Antisemitism", p. 790.

[32]   Hedges, "White Jesus and Antisemitism", p. 779.

[33]   Robin H. S. Boyd, *India and the Latin Captivity of the Church: The Cultural Context of the Gospel* (Cambridge: Cambridge University Press, 1974).

[34]   See e.g., Kwok Pui-lan, *Postcolonial Imagination and Feminist Theology* (London: SCM Press, 2005); and Joerg Rieger, *Christ & Empire: From Paul to Postcolonial Times* (Minneapolis, MN: Augsburg Fortress, 2007).

theologian is considered properly educated in many places without having engaged this misogynistic, early twentieth-century, antisemitic, Swiss theologian.[35] Who in a seminary or university in Nevada, Toronto or Belgium has been asked to read a Cameroonian theologian, unless doing specific "contextual theology"/"Third World Theology" courses? But seminarians and theology students in Nigeria, Thailand or the Bahamas will surely have a plethora of Germanic thinkers on their plates. One word explains this: colonialism. Behind colonialism, we can understand white privilege, cultural hegemony, racism, historical myopia, Orientalism, and a host of other factors.

An argument revisited: Beyond White Jesus

Previously, I suggested a way forward for rethinking Christology in this context, sketching some principles drawn from post-Shoah thought, especially that of Marianne Moyaert and Emmanuel Levinas.[36] My argument herein extends from that, and as such I will outline what these thinkers may contribute. This suggestion to revise Christology, drawing from two European thinkers (a Lithuanian–French Jewish male and a Belgian Catholic female) itself remains Western-centric, but including a female theologian as well as Jewish thought, moves beyond what typically passes for mainstream theology.[37]

Following Moyaert, when we read biblical texts and revisit the Christian tradition it means that this "must take place within a

---

[35] On Barth's antisemitism, see Hedges, *Religious Hatred*, p. 103; on his misogyny, see e.g. Yolanda Dreyer, "Karl Barth's male–female order: A kingpin of dogmatic disparity", *HTS Theological Studies* 63:4 (2007), pp. 1523–47, which argues his views on women are part of a "dehumanizing system", here at p. 1544.

[36] Hedges, "White Jesus and Antisemitism", pp. 793–5.

[37] On how non-male, non-white, non-Western theology is often bracketed out as "contextual theology", see Paul Hedges, *Controversies in Interreligious Dialogue and the Theology of Religions* (London: SCM Press, 2010), pp. 44–7; more widely on intercultural theology, pp. 44–52.

Jewish–Christian encounter 'not to Judaize Christianity, but [to end] a long Christian tradition of supersessionism'".[38] Beyond Moyaert, though, I suggest that this means seeing Jesus as a Jewish prophet because (in part), as argued, High Christology is implicated within an imperialist antisemitic legacy and so remains structurally complicit.[39] Again, following Moyaert, I lean on Levinas's notion of the Messiah who does not come, but extend beyond both Moyaert and Levinas in pursuing the Christological implications. This includes considering Rosemary Radford Ruether's question about how to square the difference between the answers to the question of whether or not the Messiah has come—to which Christians normally reply "yes", but most Jews reply "no". To quote:

> If, with Levinas, we say the Messiah does not come, then we read Jesus as of his times, a Jewish prophet, and embrace Messiahship as what we do if we live out his teachings. Here I am perhaps also exceeding Levinas's claim and taking a particular reading of being "a messiah" as an ethical imperative of all people: that is, to do the work of healing and ethical duty toward the Other.[40]

---

[38] Hedges, "White Jesus and Antisemitism", p. 793, citing Moyaert, "Who Is the Suffering Servant? A Comparative Theological Reading of Isaiah 53 After the Shoah", in Michelle Voss Roberts (ed.), *Comparing Faithfully: Insight for Systematic Theological Reflection* (New York: Fordham University Press, 2016), pp. 216–37, here at p. 231.

[39] Moreover, of course, beyond the late and out-of-kilter Johannine material, the biblical witness gives us only a human prophet/rabbi/potential messiah (but, Jewishly speaking, not a divine one, of course).

[40] Hedges, "White Jesus and Antisemitism", p. 794. It may be noted that Levinas's thought has resonances with traditional Jewish claims, and his ideas are based in a reading of the Talmud (specifically Sanhedrin 98b–99a, see also 98a). See Ephraim Meir, "Judaism and Philosophy: Each Other's Other in Levinas", *Modern Judaism: A Journal of Jewish Ideas and Experience* 30/3 (2010), pp. 348–62.

Speaking of the ethical imperative to heal the world,[41] I argue that Messiahship must be understood within the Hebrew meaning, simply to be anointed, which is—in my reading here (see below where we engage Ateek)—to have a mission within this world as an agent of justice and compassion. It is not a special title of some saviour figure coming from beyond the world. With Buber, too, we must then "act as if there were no G*d", realizing our own imperative of messianic liberative social action:

> to take the Jewish notion of Messiah seriously, as one anointed, is it not all of us who must be the agents of God's work, as Levinas proclaims in telling us that we must devote ourselves to the world? Not to (vainly) proclaim ourselves as "Messiah", but to realize that we must act in the realization of a Messianic ideal as an ethical imperative, as "a messiah" (seeing an anointed one as a person whose ethical imperative is to act righteously).[42]

Here, I will seek to further liberate our Christological thinking within the context of contemporary frames. Or, to be moved by the Spirit within our times to revivify and purify the tradition: to liberate it from itself.

A Liberationist Palestinian and Anti-Antisemitic Christology

Palestinian liberation theology is a branch of the wider tradition of Christian liberation theologies, such as the Latin American, feminist, and Black American varieties. While liberation theology is associated by some with Marxism, it should be understood as the uncovering of the biblical message of G*d's preferential option for the poor. It may be

---

[41] Here I lean on the Jewish notion of *tikkun olam*—literally: "world repair". See Gilbert Rosenthal, "Tikkun ha-Olam: The Metamorphosis of a Concept", *The Journal of Religion* 85/2 (2005), pp. 214–40; and Mark L. Winer, "*Tikkun olam*: A Jewish theology of 'repairing the world'", *Theology* 111:864 (2008), pp. 433–41.

[42] Hedges, "White Jesus and Antisemitism", p. 795.

useful to address here what may be a critique of my argument as a whole: that it takes a distinctively modern approach to rereading the Bible and Christian teaching, i.e. taking anti-racism, decolonization, and liberation as methods to reinterpret the text and tradition. Such a critique, however, would show a critical lack of awareness of how hermeneutics operates. We never interpret in a vacuum, but also within a context and a place that affects both how we see and what we see. As Gadamer tells us, as readers, we may even see things in texts that exceed what authors imagined. Within Christian thought this is clear—the later fourth-century doctrines of the Trinity were developed after only centuries, and both arose from and led to new philosophical developments and language, which were needed for these doctrines to be envisaged, for they invoked conceptions not even possible within the realm of what the biblical writers could mean by the terms "Father", "Son" and "Lady Spirit". As Lady Spirit (in Hebrew the term *ruach* is feminine[43]) guides us today, we may be inspired to read the texts consonant with a message interpreted afresh for our own age. Like a new Reformation—or the monastic revolution of the fourth century which originally rebelled against the new imperial Christianity and its seeking of power, fame, and money, or the Franciscan call to radical poverty and an embrace of nature—we may challenge the teachings and readings of the previous Christian tradition.

---

[43]   There is considerable dispute on whether the Christian Holy Spirit should be spoken of as male, female or neither, with the Greek *pneuma* being neuter, and male adjectives becoming normative, but there is considerable evidence that in Syriac and early Christian thought the Spirit was thought of as feminine, an issue raised in more recent feminist theology—as such here I use "Lady Spirit". See, variously, Anne Claar Thomasson-Rosingh, *Searching for the Holy Spirit: Feminist Theology and Traditional Doctrine* (New York: Routledge, 2015); John Dart, "Balancing Out the Trinity: The Genders of the Godhead", *Christian Century*, 16:23 (February 1983), pp. 147–50; Johannes Van Oort, "The Holy Spirit as Feminine: early Christian testimonies and their interpretation", *HTS Theological Studies* 72:1, <https://journals.co.za/doi/10.4102/hts.v72i1.3225>, accessed 16 October 2023; and Sebastian P. Brock, *The Holy Spirit in the Syrian Baptismal Tradition* (Berlin: De Gruyter, 2013), pp. 175–88.

This slight digression to justify the reading herein also points to a key revolution that Palestinian liberation theology's most famous exponent, the Anglican priest Naim Stifan Ateek, makes with regard to the older tradition of liberation, especially South American liberation theology. For other liberation theologies, the Exodus narrative is often key, with Moses's cry "Set my people free!" forming a backdrop. But the Palestinian experience of dispossession from their lands in the twentieth century in the face of what Palestinians term the *Nakba* (literally "disaster"), when with the founding of the state of Israel they were forced from their homes (Benny Morris places the number at 75,000, but acknowledges that this is a conservative estimate[44]), has uncomfortable parallels with the aftermath of Exodus. There we see genocidal biblical stories as the Israelite people claim their own home. It remains controversial to equate the current experience of the Palestinian people to the suffering under an Apartheid system, but from at least the end of the twentieth century until today the Palestinians have faced ongoing illegal occupation of their land, enforced separation of their land and people (via the separation wall), and a differential legal system in which different laws and punishments apply to them in contrast to the militant right-wing Israeli settlers who continue, often violently, to take their land with generally little repercussion. Faced with this situation, Palestinian Christians cannot neutrally read the biblical narrative of the Exodus and its entwined story of the taking of the land without seeing the parallel. Exodus, for them, is not a story of G*d's liberation. Rather, Ateek points to it being an example of militant, imperialist discourse within the biblical text—an unholy story, or one of the Bible's "texts of terror".[45]

Ateek suggests that there is a conflict between different ideas of G*d in the Hebrew Bible (I would suggest the same is true in the Newer Testament as well, and through all the Abrahamic traditions[46]), where an older tribal

---

[44]   Benny Morris, *1948: A History of the First Arab–Israeli War* (New Haven, CT and London: Yale University Press, 2008).

[45]   Phyllis Trible, *Texts of Terror: Literary–Feminist Readings of Biblical Narratives* (Minneapolis, MN: Fortress Press, 1984).

[46]   This debate is too large to enter here, but British modernist theologian Paul Badham has argued that the different conception of deity between two

deity who is vengeful and wrathful contrasts with a developing idea of a more benevolent and universal deity. Speaking of parts of 1 Samuel, Ateek avers: "Texts such as this surely reflect a primitive understanding of G*d, tribal ethics in ancient societies" which "should not be taken literally".[47] Having noted that such problematic texts are never referred to by Jesus, Ateek, quoting Richard Rohr, argues: "Basically, Jesus doesn't quote from his own Scriptures when they are punitive, imperialistic . . . classist, or exclusionary. In fact, he teaches the exact opposite in every case."[48] The message he takes from this is that: "our job as Christians is to imitate Jesus!"[49] In other words, Ateek has a Jesus-centric hermeneutic, and this justifies a stand against oppression and imperialism within other parts of the canon, while finding the message of peace and justice across both the Older and Newer Testaments.[50]

Ateek poses to all contemporary Christians a powerful and challenging question: "How can the Old Testament be the word of G*d in light of the Palestinian Christians' experience with its use to support Zionism?"[51] He is not alone, and Nur Masalha likewise states that: "In the narrative of

---

Christians in the same pew—one believing in a G*d of love and mercy who will save all, the other in a wrathful and vengeful deity who damns almost all humanity to everlasting hell fire—may be greater than that between supposedly different religious traditions; see Paul Badham, *Christian Beliefs About Life After Death* (London: SPCK, 1980), pp. 10–11.

[47] Naim Stifan Ateek, *A Palestinian Theology of Liberation: The Bible, Justice, and the Palestine–Israel Conflict* (Maryknoll, NY: Orbis, 2017), p. 53.

[48] Ateek, *A Palestinian Theology of Liberation*, p. 49, citing Richard Rohr, "How Jesus Used Scripture", *Center for Contemplation and Action* (9 February 2015). <https://cac.org/daily-meditations/jesus-used-scripture-2015–02–09/>, accessed 16 October 2023.

[49] Ateek, *A Palestinian Theology of Liberation*, p. 53, citing Rohr, "How Jesus Used Scripture".

[50] Ateek states: "The canon of this hermeneutic for Palestinian Christians is nothing less than Jesus Christ himself." See Naim Stifan Ateek, *Justice and Only Justice: A Palestinian Theology of Liberation* (Maryknoll, NY: Orbis, 1989), p. 79.

[51] Ateek, *Justice and Only Justice*, p. 78.

the Book of Exodus, there is an inextricable link between the liberation of the Israelites from slavery in Egypt and the divine mandate to plunder ancient Palestine and even commit genocide."[52] Ateek particularly draws on the way that the Amalekites, as one of the groups against whom genocide appears to be mandated, become linked in some contemporary forms of militant right-wing settler Zionism to the contemporary indigenous peoples, i.e. the Palestinians/Arabs,[53] and with reference to Deuteronomy 25:17–19 not only are they a people that G*d seemingly wants to exterminate, but "the Amalekites have come to symbolize evil and to represent the archetypical enemy of Jews".[54]

It may seem that we have strayed some way from our discussion of Christology, entering into the discussion of the hermeneutics of the Hebrew biblical text and a critique of contemporary militant forms of Zionism.[55] Yet, as we have observed, Ateek keeps a central focus in Palestinian liberation theology on seeing our tradition through the eyes of Jesus, certainly as far as we are able to do so. The Jesus whom Palestinian theologians such as Ateek help us see is a Jesus who is opposed to racism and imperialism. This Jesus highlights justice, compassion, and mercy. These are the broader frames of Palestinian liberation theology.

---

[52] Nur Masalha, "Reading the Bible with the Eyes of the Philistines, Canaanites, and Amelakites: Messianic Zionism, Zealotocracy, the Militarist Traditions of the Tanakh and the Palestinians (1967 to Gaza 2013)", in Nur Masalha and Lisa Isherwood (eds), *Theologies of Liberation in Palestine–Israel: Indigenous, Contextual, and Postcolonial Perspectives* (London: Lutterworth Press, 2014), pp. 57–114, here at p. 57.

[53] See Ateek, *A Palestinian Theology of Liberation*, p. 55, citing David K. Shipler, *Arab and Jew: Wounded Spirits in a Promised Land* (New York: Times Books, 1986), who mentions that young Yeshiva students in Kiryat Arba are "learning that today's Arabs are the Amalekites that G*d instructed the Jews 'to fight eternally and destroy'".

[54] Ateek, *A Palestinian Theology of Liberation*, p. 52.

[55] Zionism is not a singular ideology, and a critique of militant settler–colonial Zionist activity is not a critique of a Jewish desire for a homeland in Palestine. See Hedges, *Religious Hatred*, p. 118.

Ateek elucidates what he terms a seven-fold "Palestinian liberation theology of justice",[56] and we may note that justice has been identified as the key aspect of Ateek's thought.[57] These seven points are as follows. First, a *"theology of justice and love"*, with Ateek seeing these two as intertwined, with one necessitating the other, and asking us also to have love of our enemy. When we love somebody, Ateek asserts, we will respect their rights and respect them. Second, a *"theology of justice and mercy"*, which he sees as essential, but must be balanced. Justice alone may be cold and harsh, and so mercy tempers it, and he states that: "there should be no retaliation or revenge".[58] Third, a *"theology of justice and truth"*, where Ateek cites John 8:32 that "the truth will make you free", arguing we must dispel falsehoods and speak truth to power. Fourth, a *"theology of justice and security"*, where justice comes before security because a militarist realist stress on security first would be based upon force, which inherently violates the need for justice.[59] But justice is reached only when we actually have security. Fifth, a *"theology of justice and nonviolence"*, which is important to Palestinian liberation theology. Sixth, a *"theology of justice and peace"*, with the former first, but only as it leads to the latter. Emphasizing its importance he invokes Matthew 5:9: "Blessed are the peacemakers, for they will be called children of God." In Ateek's words: "Although justice is our first objective, it is only the first step toward the end of the conflict."[60] He speaks of a "dual imperative" of Palestinian Christians for a ministry that is both "prophetic and peacemaking".[61] Finally, a *"theology of justice, reconciliation, and forgiveness"*, placed in the context of healing (soteriological in liberation theology terms), where reconciliation is a first step and where there is an "acknowledgement of injustice" which can lead to "a change of attitudes and just actions",

---

[56]   Ateek, *A Palestinian Theology of Liberation*, p. 119, outlined over pp. 119–21, italics in the seven points below are in the original.

[57]   Donald Wagner, *Dying in the Land of Promise: Palestine and Palestinian Christianity from Pentecost to 2000* (London: Melisende, 2001), p. 252.

[58]   Ateek, *A Palestinian Theology of Liberation*, p. 119.

[59]   Ateek, *A Palestinian Theology of Liberation*, p. 142.

[60]   Ateek, *A Palestinian Theology of Liberation*, p. 120.

[61]   Ateek, *Justice and Only Justice*, p. 151.

but which is completed by forgiveness when it is "offered and received", meaning that "both parties are set free" from revenge (the oppressed) and guilt (the oppressor).[62] Ateek also speaks of Palestinian liberation theology having a four-fold mandate under the concepts: "*ecumenical*", "*interfaith*", "*justice and peace*", and "*international*".[63] This biblical and theological model provides us with a lens for imagining Jesus within our context; a Jesus who, I suggest, accords with the Levinasian model noted above.

I have argued: "If, with Levinas, we say the Messiah does not come, then we read Jesus as of his times, a Jewish prophet, and embrace Messiahship as what we do if we live out his teachings."[64] Our Christology is thus not about the imagined divine attributes of a celestial Jesus defined in precise Creeds, where one wrong word denotes heresy/death (When imagined as having ontic or epistemic validity, is not a Creed the utmost blasphemy: that human words, created language, can encapsulate that which transcends all words and language and human knowing?[65]) Rather, our Christology—which is Messiahology—is the living out of the justice-based example of Jesus that Ateek outlines. We may thus envisage a Palestinian liberation theology praxis-centric Messiahship which builds upon the Levinasian conception that we stand before the face of the Other with respect to justice, love, mercy, truth, security, nonviolence, peace, reconciliation, and forgiveness. Further, this notion of Messiahship may be wrapped within Ateek's four-fold mandate—ecumenical, interfaith, justice and peace, and international—which helps explain our acting in the world within a broad frame of inclusion and with a wide scope.

---

[62] Ateek, *A Palestinian Theology of Liberation*, p. 121.

[63] Ateek, *A Palestinian Theology of Liberation*, pp. 23–4, italics in original.

[64] Hedges, "White Jesus and Antisemitism", p. 794.

[65] One need not be a Kantian to question how human minds comprehend the noumenal with such precision, for the Pseudo-Dionysius and Gregory of Nazianzus provide for us the *via negativa*, alongside e.g. Aquinas, Eckhart, Marguerite Porete, Cusanus, etc. See Oliver Davies and Denys Turner (eds), *Silence and the Word: Negative Theology and Incarnation* (Cambridge: Cambridge University Press, 2008).

Palestinian liberation theology, in its critique of the Exodus narrative, also gives us a new hermeneutic: a Jesus-centric one. With this, we can address not just Christian tradition and doctrine, but also biblical texts. Texts and traditions which advocate, or embrace, racism, misogyny, imperialism, and militancy go against, as Ateek suggests, the example that Jesus gives us to follow. It therefore reinforces the critique of the White Jesus, steeped in an antisemitic imperial Christendom. Understanding Jesus, and our role in following him, is to be like the Jewish Palestinian rabbi and to share his acting—post-Shoah—as if there were no G*d, as if the Messiah does not come. It is the messiahship of *tikkun olam*,[66] or healing the earth, through the vision Ateek gives us. No messianic saviour comes from beyond, for we are the *soter*, the healer. Justice, love, mercy, truth, security, nonviolence, peace, reconciliation, and forgiveness is what we must bring to birth when we act as though no Messiah is coming.[67] This is our messianic role.

We should, perhaps, address accusations that Ateek is antisemitic and how this plays into our building an anti-antisemitic Christology. These accusations relate to the way that critique of the state of Israel can, at times, be antisemitic.[68] A careful reading of Ateek's work shows, however,

---

[66]   See note 41.

[67]   Arguably, within such a conception the Messianic Secret of Mark, and a realized eschatology, also come more clearly into focus: the title of Messiah is not one taken by Jesus alone, but also by us all as we engage in eschatology here and now as *tikkun olam*.

[68]   See the International Holocaust Remembrance Alliance (IHRA) definition of antisemitism at <https://www.holocaustremembrance.com/resources/working-definitions-charters/working-definition-antisemitism>, accessed 28 November 2023; and Paul Hedges and Luca Farrow, "Interlude 4: Can we regulate religious hatred?", in Hedges, *Religious Hatred*, pp. 195–201. Accusations of antisemitism against Ateek are not academic, but that his work "sounds no different from that of Palestinian Muslims who incite violence against Israel" has been expressed by Israeli apologists: see Chris Katulka, "Palestinian Liberation Theology", *Israel My Glory*, blog, available at: <https://israelmyglory.org/article/palestinian-liberation-theology/>, July/August 2012, accessed 25 June 2023.

that he never denies the validity of the state of Israel, nor does he accuse all Israelis, but directs critique at specific state policies and activities within a militant Zionism frame. He is explicit that this does not apply to Jews as a generic group. Some apologists for the state of Israel tend to equate any criticism of the country with antisemitism, but this is bad analysis. Ateek works with many Jews and Jewish groups for peace and reconciliation in the country. Moreover, that Palestinians wish to see Jesus as one of their own, as a Palestinian, is quite understandable. It is, arguably, no different from the way that, for instance, Black Americans under their own situation of oppression have seen the suffering Jesus as one of them.[69] This does not erase Jesus's Jewishness. When we state that Jesus was a Jewish Palestinian (from the Greco-Roman area of Palestina[70]) we do no more than refer to the evidential identity of a first century Galilean person from the countryside around Nazareth.

Towards further exploration

Here, we have moved a little further towards liberating Jesus from the Latin, imperial, colonial, White, antisemitic, racist entrapment through which we so often receive him. Is it our role to liberate (save) Jesus? Perhaps the only way we can be saved/healed—liberated from our false vision—is when we first liberate Jesus. Then, the anti-racist Jesus of justice can reveal himself to us, but revealed in our own being and action. If we embrace the Jewish Palestinian Jesus that Ateek teaches us, it seems

---

[69] See Cone, *Black Theology*. Notably, before Cone the concept was raised by the poet Langston Hughes in his 1931 poem "Christ in Alabama"; see Lilian Calles Barger, "The Strange Fruit of American Religion", USIH Blog (2018), <https://s-usih.org/2018/08/the-strange-fruit-of-american-religion/>, accessed 16 October 2023.

[70] At different periods, Rome reorganized its system and naming of provinces and administrative districts around Judea, with the whole region becoming Syria-Palaestina in the second century CE. See G. M. FitzGerald, "Palestine in the Roman Period, 63 B.C.–A.D. 324", *Palestine Exploration Quarterly* 88:1 (1956), pp. 38–48.

that the Spirit moves us to see anew, in a new Reformation, to become a truly messianic people. My argument here may shock, may even seem heretical. But, rather, the blasphemy is the imperialist, antisemitic, racist, White Jesus of tradition. This is what we, with Lady Spirit, should oppose.

Afterword: Towards a Hopeful Future

Alan Race and Jonathan Clatworthy

Christ, the Creeds, and Liberal Theology

This book, as the Introduction explains, has its roots in a series of lectures celebrating the centenary of a controversial conference at Girton College, Cambridge in 1921. That conference was held by the Churchmen's Union, later renamed the Modern Churchmen's Union and now Modern Church.

Looking back on the last century, what has changed? One major change is that theologians and churches have moved in different directions. Theologians are now more aware of how often Christian voices have sung the tunes of imperialism, patriarchy, and triumphalism—and have thereby promoted wars of aggression, colonialism, the oppression of women, antisemitism, and the dismissal or even demonization of ethnic minority and different non-white cultures, as well as other faith traditions. But, as this book has illustrated, there are alternatives.

Churches have moved in a different direction. Today what strikes the reader of those century-old debates is that we now argue about different things: then, it was the divinity of Christ, but now, it is how Christ can be identified as the instigator of a transformed multicultural and multireligious world. Yet the horrified responses to the analyses of the divinity of Christ sound just like today's horrified responses to the liberal questioning of, say, a physical resurrection of Jesus, or of miracles as interventions by God in natural processes, or of the refusal to recognize same-sex partnerships and gender transition. We still hear demands that any deviation from inherited teachings is good reason for sacking a bishop, or even a priest. For some, what matters is to protect the purity of the institution as currently conceived, perhaps under the threat of schism.[1] For others, like the spokespeople of Modern Church, what matters is the search for truth according to theological considerations in dialogue with the best insights from the natural and social sciences, philosophy, and cultural studies.

Christ

With respect to Christology, we have seen how the Girton conference speakers recognized the influence of Hellenistic polytheism on early Christian texts. This influence has now been virtually forgotten in much church, and even theological, discourse. It is difficult to imagine the matter being raised today without an even greater furore.

Yet we know people are influenced—even shaped—by their culture. Just as Europeans today are influenced by American culture, often without noticing it, so also first-century Jews might think of themselves as committed to the god of the Hebrew scriptures without noticing that they were also taking for granted some of the conflicting theologies of Hellenistic polytheism. An evangelical Christian today may be committed to living "biblically", while also having a bank account that relies on usury which is seriously frowned on in biblical texts. Such a person may notice the apparent inconsistency and find a way to justify it; or may notice it and not care; or may not even notice it. Refusing to face inconsistencies properly could also be a feature of some New Testament epistles. For example, Ephesians and Colossians refer to "cosmic powers of this present darkness", "spiritual forces of evil in the heavenly places",[2] "things visible and invisible, whether thrones or dominions or rulers or powers", "elemental spirits of the universe"[3]—references in letters written to congregations in Greek-speaking cities, Jews and Greek sympathizers with Judaism, who were in principle loyal to the Jewish scriptures but also steeped in concepts involving Hellenistic polytheism. Whether and how first-century Christians negotiated the tension will no doubt have

---

[1]   This, for example, is the position of the Global Anglican Future Conference (GAFCON), <https://www.gafcon.org/>, accessed 16 October 2023.

[2]   Ephesians 6:12.

[3]   Colossians 1:16 and 2:8, 20. Cf. Romans 8:38–9.

varied from person to person, just as it does today since the same issue arises for us.

We can distinguish three background influences on passages in the pages of the New Testament associated with Christological reflections. The first is the practice of honouring a human being in a manner appropriate to the divine. Hellenistic cities contained many voluntary associations where members had some interests in common. They would gather for a meal from time to time and the event would begin with a libation poured to the patron, who was either a god or a human person praised for a memorable activity. This would be accompanied with a statement recalling the patron's significance. Athenians in Rome, for example, might honour Theseus for saving Athens by killing the Minotaur. In Hellenistic culture, unlike the Jewish tradition, the distinction between divine and human realities was fuzzier. It was a short step to grant a human patron some divine-like status which could be left quite vague.

The followers of Jesus in Hellenistic cities could adapt their eucharists along these lines. While the reasons they expressed for honouring Jesus would presumably have varied, Hellenistic culture would naturally have pointed towards describing him as a bit like Theseus, as a bringer of salvation. The resurrection could then be seen, in a manner familiar to both Hellenistic polytheists and Jews, as divine vindication of a loyal martyr. In this context, the extent to which Jesus was seen as divine did not need to be specified, and no doubt varied.[4]

Our main source for this development of the Eucharist is Paul's epistles. Where he focuses specifically on eucharistic procedure he complains that their unequal sharing of food misses the principle of equality in the Christian community.[5] We can see here a tension between normal Hellenistic practice and the Christian purpose of eucharistic sharing.

A second contribution to New Testament Christology was the attribution of divine fatherhood to famous people. In the first century CE, the claim was most often made for Alexander the Great and Augustus. Suetonius described Augustus's conception as follows:

---

[4]   Burton Mack, *A Myth of Innocence: Mark and Christian Origins* (Philadelphia, PA: Fortress Press, 1988), pp. 81, 111 and 119.

[5]   1 Corinthians 11:17–34.

Then there is a story which I found in a book called *Theologumena*, by Asclepias of Mendes. Augustus's mother, Atia, with certain married women friends, once attended a solemn midnight service at the Temple of Apollo, where she had her litter set down, and presently fell asleep as the others also did. Suddenly a serpent glided up, entered her, and then glided away again. On awakening, she purified herself, as if after intimacy with her husband. An irremovable coloured mark in the shape of a serpent, which then appeared on her body, made her ashamed to visit the public baths any more; and the birth of Augustus nine months later suggested a divine paternity. Atia dreamed that her intestines were carried up to Heaven and overhung all lands and sea; and Octavius, that the sun rose from between her thighs.

Augustus' birth coincided with the Senate's famous debate on the Catilinarian conspiracy, and when Octavius arrived late, because of Atia's confinement, Publius Nigidius Figulus the astrologer, hearing at what hour the child had been delivered, cried out: "The ruler of the world is now born." Everyone believes this story.[6]

The birth narratives in Matthew and Luke[7] similarly indicate that Jesus had a human mother and a divine father. The clearly expressed role of the snake makes Augustus more definitely semi-divine than Jesus, since the Gospel writers valued Mary's virginal conception; otherwise the evangelists' birth narratives breathe the same air. Despite New Testament references to Joseph being the father of Jesus,[8] Jesus's divine conception has remained an influential doctrine.[9]

A third background influence on New Testament Christology is that gods in the ancient world could appear for a while in human form before

---

[6]   Suetonius, *The Twelve Caesars*, tr. Robert Graves (Harmondsworth: Penguin, 1957), 94.4, p. 101.

[7]   Matthew 1–2; Luke 1:1–2:39.

[8]   Matthew 1:16; 13:54–6; Luke 3:23–4; Romans 1:1–4.

[9]   See Marcus J. Borg and John Dominic Crossan, *What the Gospels Really Teach About Jesus's Birth* (New York: HarperCollins Publishers, 2007).

returning to the heavens. Just as in Suetonius's story cited above where Apollo took the form of a snake, gods were also capable of appearing in the form of a human being. The New Testament book which comes closest to treating Jesus in this way is the Gospel of John. It was no accident that John's Gospel became a major source for the increasing divinizing of Jesus under the metaphysical conditions of Greek philosophy in the early Christian centuries.[10]

There was, therefore, a variety of first-century models paving the way for the later credal affirmation of the divinity of Christ. In 1921, the Girton speakers could discuss these openly, asking what could be believed in their own day. We have seen how they were opposed by theological and ecclesiastical forces from the start, in a mood more determined to close down debate than to refute the arguments. It is difficult to imagine that Church leaders today would respond any differently.

Creeds

The fate of the Creeds tells a similar story. The Church of England's 1662 *Book of Common Prayer* mandates the recitation of the Nicene Creed at every Holy Communion service.[11] The Girton speakers could discuss what its purpose is and whether we should have Creeds at all. Nevertheless, the 1662 instruction remained unchanged in the 1980 *Alternative Service Book*[12] and virtually unchanged in the 2000 *Common Worship* liturgical revisions. The only difference is that its replacement by

---

10 Cf. the comment by John Dominic Crossan that God's dream for a world of justice and peace "was always *with* God and *was* God. But, John claims, it became embodied, incarnated, revealed humanly in Jesus . . . " in *The Power of Parable: How Fiction by Jesus Became Fiction about Jesus* (New York: HarperCollins, 2012), p. 225.

11 The Church of England, *The Book of Common Prayer and Administration of the Sacraments and other Rites and Ceremonies of the Church* (Oxford: Oxford University Press, 1662), p. 240.

12 Church of England Central Board of Finance, *Alternative Service Book* (London: Clowes, SPCK, 1980), pp. 123 and 181.

the Apostles' Creed or the Athanasian Creed is permitted "on occasions".[13] No other British organization expects everybody present to stand up and recite a statement of belief. Such public recitation presupposes that all present should believe the same things, and as such is a fossil of imperial theology.

Of course the regulars know the rules. Nobody obliges churchgoers to know or care whether they actually believe what the Creeds state. But enquirers and newcomers rightly expect that if people stand up in public to make a statement, they do believe it.

So why are churches still so wedded to Creeds? Maybe it is partly intellectual laziness: "this is what we have always done". Maybe it is also about control: when your car needs repair you may take it to mechanics and grant them control over it because of their knowledge. In the same way, Church leaders who claim to uphold "traditional" teaching can enjoy a kind of psychological control over Christians who feel they ought to believe it but do not really understand it. As the philosopher and social anthropologist, Ernest Gellner, noted:

> Unintelligibility leaves the disciple with a secret guilt of not understanding or not avowing it, or both, which binds him to the master who is both responsible for it and seems untainted by it. The belief that the naked emperor is clothed is better social cement than that a naked one is naked—or even that a clothed one is clothed.[14]

---

[13]   Church House Publishing, *Common Worship: Services and Prayers for the Church of England* (London: Church House Publishing, 2000), pp. 138, 173, 213 and 234.

[14]   Ernest Gellner, "Is belief really necessary?", in *The Devil in Modern Philosophy Vol. 3* (London: Routledge & Kegan Paul, first pub. 1974), and reprinted in I. C. Jarvie and J. Agassi (eds), *The Devil in Modern Philosophy Vol. 3* (London: Routledge & Kegan Paul, 2003), Chapter 5. Also cited in Mary Beard, *Pagan Priests: Religion and Power in the Ancient World* (London: Duckworth, 1990), p. 189.

Liberal Theology since 1921

In the 1920s, Modernism was a diverse and popular movement, especially influential in art and architecture. Modernist theology meant much the same as liberal theology, though the word "Liberal" was more associated with German Protestantism and "Modernist" with Catholic renewal movements. "Liberalism" now has a wider range of meanings, but then, for the Churchmen's Union, "liberal theology" meant the willingness to question inherited teachings—thus bringing theology into line with every other discipline of study.

Modernism, with its liberal theology, did enable Christian thought to be opened up in the churches. The publication of John Robinson's *Honest to God* in 1963 was something of a watershed in this respect.[15] For many it held open the door to a credible, rational account of the divine stripped of unconvincing dogmas. For others, and for the same reason, it was the last straw—especially as it came so soon after the 1962 introduction of the contraceptive pill, an innovation provoking the fury of many Church leaders.

Behind the reaction was an influential philosophical issue. In the 1920s, the Vienna Circle had produced the theory of logical positivism. Its central claim was the Verification Principle, according to which any statement which cannot be verified either empirically (by observation) or analytically (by mathematical or logical deduction) was meaningless. Whereas their nineteenth-century positivist predecessors had argued that God, not being observable, should be deemed non-existent, the Verification Principle rendered the very idea of God meaningless. In philosophical circles the Verification Principle was soon refuted, but it reached its height of popularity in the 1950s and 1960s.[16] It seemed as though the spirit of rational enquiry beloved of Modernists had led, after all, to the atheism they were trying to oppose.

Many clergy began to doubt their faith, sensing that religion's time was up. The Modern Churchmen's Union proved a safe haven for them, with its unafraid commitment to the search for truth. Accepting them

---

[15]   John A. T. Robinson, *Honest to God* (London: SCM Press, 1963).

[16]   Oswald Hanfling, *Essential Readings in Logical Positivism* (Oxford: Blackwell, 1981).

into membership changed the Union's character. It could seem attractive not for what it said but for what it refused to say—less a thinker's defence of believing, more a churchgoer's defence of unbelieving. To more committed atheists it might seem like a cigarette filter, designed to take the most poisonous bits out but still put there to encourage the bad habit of religion. While there still are those who lose their faith and like to meet up with fellow-travellers, providing a religious society for those giving up religion does not have a better prognosis than providing a tennis court for people who have given up tennis.

To evangelicals, meanwhile, liberal theology could seem like "atheism for churchgoers". The recent evangelical revival began in the 1960s. "The great movement of renewal was undoubtedly April 1967—the National Evangelical Congress at Keele", wrote Adrian Hastings.[17] Hastings continues: "It was the first deliberate and public step towards closing the mental schism with most other Christians which Evangelicals had been somewhat smugly cultivating ever since 1910."[18] Under the leadership of John Stott, the Evangelical revival reacted against both atheism and liberal theology, lumping them together as though they were the same thing. The changing mood in the Modern Churchmen's Union was, of course, grist to their mill.

So there was an opening up, but then a closing down. In the 1960s, neither side foresaw the decline of atheist conviction. Both its logical positivist foundation and its Marxist clothing were on the wane. Public opinion, which had seen the rise of atheism for 150 years (and longer in France)[19] began to turn away from the empty world where everything is

---

[17] Adrian Hastings, *A History of English Christianity 1920–1985* (London: Collins, 1986), p. 553.

[18] Ibid., p. 554.

[19] Gavin Hyman, *Short History of Atheism* (London and New York: I. B. Tauris, 2010). The word "atheism" had a wider meaning before the seventeenth century. It was applied to those who did not do or believe what was expected of them, and would now be described as heretics or deists. Michael J. Buckley S. J., *At the Origins of Modern Atheism* (New Haven, CT and London: Yale University Press, 1987); Jan Bremmer, "Atheism in Antiquity", in Michael Martin (ed.), *The Cambridge Companion to Atheism* (Cambridge: Cambridge

available for scientific measurement and control, and instead longed for transcendence. Countless new spiritual movements evolved. The one which did not grow was Christianity. There, the Evangelical revival had been so successful that it was widely seen as the only authoritative voice of Christianity. The teachings of John Stott and Jim Packer, with their black-and-white distinctions between heaven-bound true Christians and the hell-bound majority, and their many instructions about what true Christians should do and believe,[20] were exactly the kind of thing New Agers and other spiritual seekers were determined to avoid. In this way the Evangelical revival did more than any other movement to repel spiritual seekers.[21]

The effect on public opinion can be seen by comparing 1921 with today. The Girton conference made front page news. Admittedly, Cyril Emmet later wrote: "For some reason the attention of the press was attracted; it was a slack season and the public was waiting for the arrival of Charlie Chaplin."[22] Nevertheless what the Church taught, and the debates about what it taught, were of interest to the British majority. Today no national newspaper would bother to report the proceedings of such a theological society.

University Press, 2007), pp. 11–20; David Wootton, "New Histories of Atheism", in Michael Hunter and David Wootton (eds), *Atheism from the Reformation to the Enlightenment* (Oxford: Clarendon, 1992), pp. 25–51.

[20]   Most popular was John Stott, *The Cross of Christ* (Leicester: IVP, 1986). Also, J. I. Packer, *Knowing God* (London: Hodder & Stoughton, 1973).

[21]   See for example, Harriet Harris, *Fundamentalism and Evangelicals* (Oxford: Clarendon, 1998).

[22]   Cyril W. Emmet, "The Modernist Movement in the Church of England", *Journal of Religion* 2/6 (November 1922), p. 565.

Looking to the future

Church hierarchies, worrying about declining numbers, are still inclined to see the Evangelical revival as the model for growth in church attendance. Easiest to applaud are the superficialities—the popular style of music, the informal dress and worship, the individualist "me" theology, the absence of any critique of inherited teaching. Whereas the issues raised at Girton in 1921 are still debated by academic theologians, Church leaders have largely lost interest in them.[23]

We could easily conclude that Modernism and its spirit of free enquiry has been effectively suppressed in the churches. Nevertheless the theology represented by that conference, and by the wider movement it represented, has proved its worth. Time and time again—on biblical interpretation, on doctrinal criticism, on evolution, on matters of sexual ethics, on the state's penal policy, on women priests and bishops—its open-minded willingness to engage with new evidence and new insights has meant that despite countless official disapprovals it has usually ended up winning the arguments.

Modern Western culture has over the last 50 years emerged from a century and a half of religious pessimism. During that time, many believed that religious faith had been, or would be, disproved by science. The main Christian denominations became defensive and counter-cultural. They developed reactionary doctrines. Instead of judging new theories on their merits they often exulted in culture-defying older beliefs and turned them into essential dogmas. They thus established the tradition of insisting that in order to count as a Christian, or as a member of a particular church, one must believe certain things which nobody else believes. Whether it was the Virgin Birth, or Jesus walking on water, or a six-day creation, or the immorality of remarriage after divorce, or homosexuality, a variety

---

[23]   Cf. the account by Andrew Brown and Linda Woodhead, *That Was The Church That Was: How the Church of England Lost the English People* (London: Bloomsbury Continuum, 2016).

of doctrines were refashioned into defiant symbols of Christian loyalty over against the big bad world.[24]

This stance still motivates a great many churches and theologians. Today, however, far from defending Christianity against its greatest threat, it has itself become the greatest threat. To treat those symbols as essential to Christian believing only makes sense to those who were brought up with them. To others, to insist on them now is to tell enquirers that they are not welcome unless they are prepared to engage with past traditions of petty in-fighting. As Jane Harrison observed in 1921: "The hot emotion of one generation is the cold authority of the next."[25]

To the extent that the explorations in this book point the way to a more hopeful future, we might expect them to have the following features:

1. Truth and Reason

Revelation is not opposed to reason, but is acquired through it. Many people do receive uninvited religious and mystical experiences, and their lives are often greatly affected by them,[26] but to derive propositions of Christian truth from them requires reasoning processes. Every item of Christian teaching can therefore be legitimately questioned.

Our searchings must not be hindered by dogmas. There always have been people who want to puzzle out the questions that face them, and other people more concerned to establish who they belong with and what they must believe in order to belong. The commitment to truth should govern the rules of our institutions, not the other way round. We all accept that this should be the case in medicine, in mathematics, in

---

[24] For introductions to this trend, see Darrell Jodock (ed.), *Catholicism Contending with Modernity: Roman Catholic Modernism and Anti-Modernism in Historical Context* (Cambridge: Cambridge University Press, 2000), and D. W. Bebbington, *Evangelicalism in Modern Britain: A History from the 1730s to the 1980s* (London: Routledge, 1989).

[25] *Modern Churchman* 11:4 (1921), p. 414.

[26] Marianne Rankin, *An Introduction to Religious and Spiritual Experience* (London: Continuum, 2008), provides an impressive collection and analysis of many accounts and reports. Also of abiding interest is J. M. Cohen and J-F. Phipps, *The Common Experience* (London: Rider & Company, 1979).

economic policy, and elsewhere. When it turns out not to be the case, we invariably disapprove. We should find the courage to insist on the same principles for theology.

2. Jesus

The second dominant feature of this book is a concentration on the humanity of the human being, Jesus. All theories about Christ should be based on the man Jesus, taking full account of his context in first century Galilee. Far too often Christian theology has offered a free-floating heavenly Christ without any worldly moorings. A Christ like that has often been too easily moulded to suit the loudest voices of the day, and has thereby justified antisemitism, patriarchy, imperialism, and whatever else the most powerful wished to promote.

Whether Christological discussion centres on the philosophical problem of how humanity might reveal divine purpose and presence, or on the urgent problems facing humanity as a global whole, it is from within the humanity of Jesus that Christian insight into transcendent reality arises. After all, this is what is presented through the Christian gospel tradition, through human stories of Jesus's encounters, through his determined message of the Kingdom of God, and through his empathy with human suffering and sharp confrontations with religious and political authorities. But in terms of a developing story of Christology the humanity of Jesus has struggled to be fully integrated within the one person. What seems so obvious and necessary for us today has not always been the case. We might ask: why were there agonizing debates in the early centuries over the question of whether or not Jesus actually possessed a human soul?[27] The question itself is one significant measure of the contextual difference between then and now.

The question that now dominates Christological discussion is the soteriological one: what does it mean to call Jesus "saviour" or "liberator"? And the answers will depend on context—whether they be social–political, or spiritual–existential, or multireligious. These contexts

---

[27]   See the helpful discussion in Maurice Wiles, "The Nature of the Early Debate about Christ's Human Soul", *Working Papers in Doctrine* (London: SCM Press, 1976), Chapter 5.

too are reflected in the various chapters of this book. When Natalie presses the Jesus question in the Gospels, "Who do you say that I am?", the answer will not be simply a title—Son of God, Saviour, Prophet, Son of Man etc.—but will need to incorporate a sense of how it is that Jesus makes a difference in different contexts, secular and religious.

3. Context and Change

New insights have a habit of appearing unexpectedly, and coming from unexpected sources. We have learned how historical context has shaped beliefs and practices. Many new ideas do not pass the test of time, but some do. Rather than treating change as a threat, Christians can be confident enough to welcome it. Regarding context, historical analysis shows that Christian faith, and therefore reflection on "Christ", has meant different things at different times. Faith in the third century reflected different interests, assumptions, pressures, and possibilities, than did faith in the tenth, or sixteenth, or twentieth centuries. Development through change has never been a smooth process and faith has never stayed still—it did not arrive ready-made in first-century Palestine.[28] Context affects content, and it is theology's job to wrestle with the ramifications.

This view of Christological reflection is the driving force behind what is probably the most comprehensive study of Christology published in the last 25 years, the American Jesuit Roger Haight's *Jesus: Symbol of God*. Embracing the Second Vatican Council's theological method of "inculturation"—which is equivalent to what we have termed "contextualization"—and referring to a milestone conference of the General Congregation of Jesuits from around the world, Haight writes: "Inculturation is treated as the incarnation of Christian faith and life within the diversity of human experiences that are codified in the languages, ideas, values and behavioural patterns that make up a culture or subculture."[29] This book's title *What Christ? Whose Christ?* consciously

---

[28]   Cf. Alan Race, *My Journey as a Religious Pluralist: A Christian Theology of Religions Reclaimed* (Eugene, OR: Resource Publications, Wipf & Stock, 2021), Part One: Critical Foundations, pp. 3–36.

[29]   Roger Haight, S. J., *Jesus: Symbol of God* (Maryknoll, NY: Orbis Press, 1999), p. xi. Haight is referring to the conference documents in John L. McCarthy

illustrates the challenges presented by inculturation/contextualization and the authors accept its framing for exploring their different subject matters. They make clear that context really does affect Christology's content. This is not to say that context *determines* content, but that only the recognition of the historic dynamic between content and context has the potential to render faith meaningful for new times and places. As Haight, again citing the Jesuit conference, reports it: "In a predominantly secular context, our faith and our understanding of faith are often freed from contingent cultural complications and, as a result, purified and deepened."[30] This is a hope-filled observation and a number of the essays in this book echo it by speaking of liberating Christ from captivity to superannuated thought-forms and imperial pretensions.

The Girton speakers were right to challenge their inherited dogmas, and we are right to challenge them today. Two thousand years after Jesus began his movement, a quarter of the world's population count themselves as his followers. This makes Christianity the biggest social movement in the whole of human history. How did that happen?[31] Was it because 400 years after his death an ecumenical council finally produced an adequate definition of Jesus's divine status? Or was it because millions through the centuries praised him in the highest language they had, because he had brought them hope?

What Christ? Whose Christ? offers a resource for readers to undertake their own journey of hope.

(ed.), "Our Mission and Culture", *Documents of the Thirty-Fourth General Congregation of the Society of Jesus* (St Louis, MO: The Institute of Jesuit Sources, 1995), #3.

[30] Cited by Haight, *Jesus*, p. xii.

[31] An interesting account is given in Bart D. Ehrman, *The Triumph of Christianity: How a Forbidden Religion Swept the World* (London: Oneworld Publications, 2018).

Contributors

Mark D. Chapman is Vice-Principal of Ripon College Cuddesdon and Professor of the History of Modern Theology at the University of Oxford. An Anglican priest and Canon Theologian of Truro Cathedral, he has worked in many different areas of modern theology and Church history. He has written and edited over 30 books, including *Theology at War and Peace: English Theology and Germany in the First World War* (Routledge, 2017); *Theology and Society in Three Cities: Berlin, Oxford and Chicago, 1800–1914* (James Clarke, 2014); *Anglican Theology* (T&T Clark, 2012).

Jonathan Clatworthy is a retired Anglican priest and tutor in Theology, Ethics and Philosophy. He has been General Secretary of Modern Church. His books relate to his main research interest, the relationship between monotheism and ethics. Among his publications are *Liberal Faith in a Divided Church* (O Books, 2008) and *Why Progressives Need God: An Ethical Defence of Monotheism* (Christian Alternative, 2017).

Alan Race is an Anglican priest–theologian, and has authored and edited a number of books and articles on Interfaith Theology and Dialogue. His most recent book is *My Journey as a Religious Pluralist: A Christian Theology of Religions Reclaimed* (Wipf & Stock, 2021). He was Chair of the Modern Church Trustees (2017–22) and continues as Chair of the World Congress of Faiths.

Natalie K. Watson is a theologian, writer, and editor based in Peterborough, England. She has a doctorate in theology from Durham University, and is the author of several books and articles on feminist theology, including *Introducing Feminist Ecclesiology* (Continuum, 2002) and *Feminist Theology* (Eerdmans, 2003).

Anantanand Rambachan is Emeritus Professor of Religion at Saint Olaf College in Minnesota, United States. Rambachan has been involved in interreligious relations and dialogue for over 40 years as a Hindu contributor and analyst. His most recent book is *Pathways to Hindu–Christian Dialogue* (Fortress Press, 2022).

Mathias Schneider is Postdoctoral Research Fellow at the Center for Religion and Modernity and interim chair at the Institute for Religious Studies and Intercultural Theology at the University of Münster. He has recently published a monograph *Buddhist Interpretations of Jesus: A Religious-Historical and Theological Study* (TVZ Zurich, 2023). His main research interests are Buddhist–Christian relations, Comparative Theology, Christology, Eschatology, interreligious dialogue, and the theology of religions.

Paul Hedges is Associate Professor at SRP, RSIS, Nanyang Technological University, Singapore. He has published 14 books and over 80 academic papers. His latest books are: *Understanding Religion: Theories and Methods for Studying Religiously Diverse Societies* (University of California Press, 2021) and *Religious Hatred: Prejudice, Islamophobia, and Antisemitism in Global Context* (Bloomsbury Publishing, 2021).

Milton Keynes UK
Ingram Content Group UK Ltd.
UKHW020800290524
443401UK00009B/98